Stand Out 1
Grammar Challenge
Second Edition

HEINLE
CENGAGE Learning

Australia • Brazil • Japan • Korea • Mexico • Singapore • Spain • United Kingdom • United States

Stand Out 1 Grammar Challenge
Rob Jenkins and Staci Johnson

Publisher: Sherrise Roehr

Acquisitions Editor: Tom Jefferies

Director of Content and Media Production:
  Michael Burggren

Development Editor: Michael Ryall

Product Marketing Manager: Katie Kelley

Sr. Content Project Editor: Maryellen E. Killeen

Sr. Print Buyer: Mary Beth Hennebury

Development Editor: Carol Crowell

Project Manager: Tunde A. Dewey

Cover / Text Designer: Studio Montage

Compositor: Parkwood Composition
  Service, Inc.

© 2009 Heinle, Cengage Learning

For permission to use material from this text or product,
submit all requests online at **cengage.com/permissions**
Further permissions questions can be emailed to
permissionrequest@cengage.com

ISBN 10: 1-4240-0987-1
ISBN 13: 978-1-4240-0987-9

Heinle
25 Thomson Place
Boston, MA 02210
USA

Cengage Learning is a leading provider of customized learning solutions with
office locations around the globe, including Singapore, the United Kingdom,
Australia, Mexico, Brazil and Japan. Locate our local office at:
international.cengage.com/region

Cengage Learning products are represented in Canada
by Nelson Education, Ltd.

Visit Heinle online at **elt.heinle.com**
Visit our corporate website at **cengage.com**

Printed in Canada
1 2 3 4 5 6 7 8 9 10   11 10 09 08

CONTENTS

TO THE TEACHER

Stand Out 1 Grammar Challenge challenges students to develop and expand their grammar skills through fifty-nine guided exercises or "challenges."

Each Challenge includes:

▶ **Charts** Clear grammar charts help the teacher lay out the components of structures and provide useful example sentences.

▶ **Notes** Notes within the charts help students understand important shifts in language use and meaning through concise explanations.

▶ **Practice** Exercises challenge students to master grammar structures while reviewing the vocabulary and thematic contexts actively taught in *Stand Out 1 Student Book*. Additional exercises reinforce grammar structures passively introduced in *Stand Out 1 Student Book* contexts.

How to use the *Stand Out 1 Grammar Challenge* workbook

The *Stand Out 1 Grammar Challenge* workbook can be used in a variety of ways:

- The grammar challenges can be assigned daily or on an as-needed basis.

- The grammar challenges can be completed individually, with a partner, or as a class.

- Students may complete challenges at home or in the classroom.

- Instructors can provide guided feedback upon completion, or ask students to self-correct or peer-edit. All exercises are formatted to provide for ease of correction and assessment.

- The *Grammar Challenge 1* answer key is available to teachers on the *Stand Out* website at: **standout.heinle.com**. It can be printed out for student use.

- The grammar challenges need not be followed in any particular order within a unit. Some challenges will be review for students, while others will reinforce the newer structures from *Stand Out 1 Student Book*.

- The *Stand Out 1 Grammar Challenge* workbook is an effective supplement in a multi-level classroom because it challenges the highly motivated students while providing support for students who need extra reinforcement.

The appendix includes a glossary of grammar terms with examples. This is intended as a reference for both students and teachers, but it is not intended that all these terms will be understood at this level. The appendix also includes grammar charts from the *Stand Out 1 Grammar Challenge* workbook as well as lists of irregular verbs and verb conjugations.

However you choose to use it, you'll find that the *Stand Out 1 Grammar Challenge* workbook is a flexible and effective grammar tool for teachers and students seeking challenging grammar instruction.

Welcome to Our Class

CHALLENGE 1 ➤ The Verb *Be*

A Read the conversation.

Roberto: Hi. I'm Roberto. What's your name?
Gabriela: My name is Gabriela.
Roberto: Welcome to our class.
Gabriela: Thank you.
Roberto: Our teacher is Miss Jones.

B Write the names of four students in your class.

	What's your name?
1.	
2.	
3.	
4.	

C Read the chart.

The Verb *Be* in Greetings				
Greeting	Subject	*Be*	Your name	Example sentence
hi	I	am	Hans	Hi. I **am** Hans. (I'm Hans.)
hello	my name	is	Maria	Hello. My name **is** Maria.
				Hello. My name**'s** Maria.

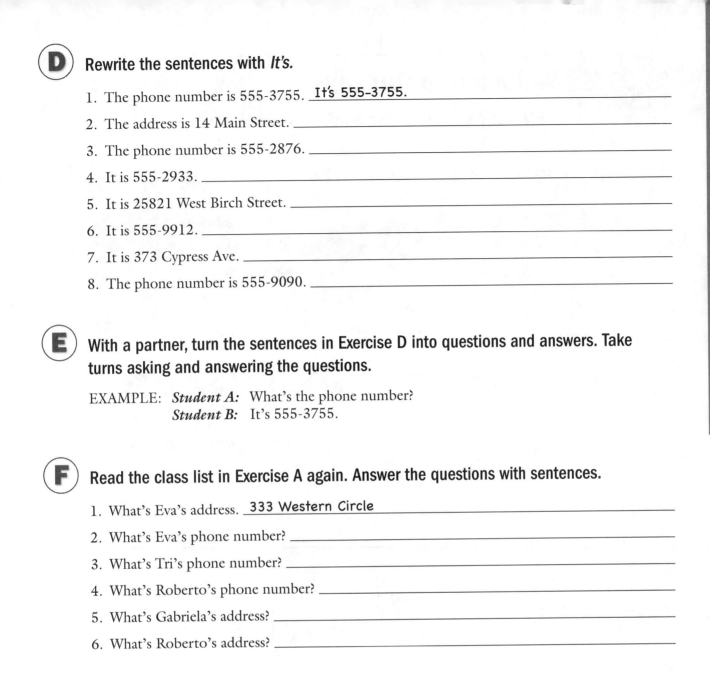

D Rewrite the sentences with *It's*.

1. The phone number is 555-3755. <u>It's 555-3755.</u>

2. The address is 14 Main Street. _____

3. The phone number is 555-2876. _____

4. It is 555-2933. _____

5. It is 25821 West Birch Street. _____

6. It is 555-9912. _____

7. It is 373 Cypress Ave. _____

8. The phone number is 555-9090. _____

E With a partner, turn the sentences in Exercise D into questions and answers. Take turns asking and answering the questions.

EXAMPLE: *Student A:* What's the phone number?
            Student B: It's 555-3755.

F Read the class list in Exercise A again. Answer the questions with sentences.

1. What's Eva's address. <u>333 Western Circle</u>

2. What's Eva's phone number? _____

3. What's Tri's phone number? _____

4. What's Roberto's phone number? _____

5. What's Gabriela's address? _____

6. What's Roberto's address? _____

G Answer the questions with *It's*.

1. What's your address? _____

2. What's your phone number? _____

3. What's a friend's address? _____

4. What's a friend's phone number? _____

Welcome to Our Class

CHALLENGE 3 ➤ Imperatives (Action Verbs)

A Match the words and the pictures. Write the letter.

_e_ 1. a name   a.    d.

____ 2. paper

____ 3. a student   b.    e.

____ 4. a book

____ 5. a teacher   c.

B Read the chart.

Imperatives			
Subject	**Verb**	**Information**	**Example sentence**
~~you~~	stand up		**Stand up.**
~~you~~	sit down		**Sit down.**
~~you~~	take out	a piece of paper	**Take out** a piece of paper.
~~you~~	open	the book	**Open** the book.
~~you~~	listen to	the teacher	**Listen to** the teacher.
~~you~~	write	your name	**Write** your name.
~~you~~	help	a student	**Help** a student.
~~you~~	read	a book	**Read** a book.

Imperatives (Action Verbs)

Circle the correct word or words.

1. _____.	Stand up	Stands up	stood up
2. _____ your books.	open	opens	Open
3. _____ the paper.	Reads	reading	Read
4. _____ the teacher.	Listen to	listens to	Listens to
5. _____ your name.	Open	sit down	Write
6. _____ a piece of paper.	Take out	open	Listen
7. _____ a student.	Stand up	Help	Sit down
8. _____	stands up	Sit down.	Sits Down

 Look at the pictures. Write the action verb.

1.

open

2.

stood up

3.

_____

4.

stood up

5.

_____

6.

_____

7.

_____

8.

_____

E **Give directions to a partner.**

1. Open the book to page 65.
2. Read page 65.
3. Stand up.
4. Sit down.

5. Listen to the teacher.
6. Take out a piece of paper.
7. Write your name.

UNIT 1 Talking with Others

CHALLENGE 1 ➤ Simple Present: Be

A Look at the information.

married	33 years old	*divorced*	**China**
	single	Russia	15
75 years old		**England**	

B Write the words from Exercise A in the correct column.

Marital status	Age	Country

C Read the chart.

Simple Present: Be			
Subject	Be	Information	Example sentence
I	am	43 years old	I **am** 43 years old. (I'm 43 years old.)
he she	is	single from Argentina from Russia married	He **is** single. (Roberto **is** single.) She **is** from Argentina.
we you they	are		We **are** single. You **are** married. They **are** from Russia.

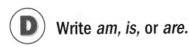

D **Write *am*, *is*, or *are*.**

1. She _____is_____ from San Diego.

2. We _____ 35 years old.

3. They _____ from Chicago.

4. I _____ divorced.

5. You _____ married.

6. He _____ 12 years old.

7. John _____ from Honduras.

8. Pedro and Maria _____ married.

9. Jennifer and I _____ from the U.S.

10. Anabel _____ divorced.

11. The students _____ from Cuba.

12. The teacher _____ from Canada.

E **Circle the correct answers.**

1. Where are you from?

    a. I am from China.

    b. I'm China.

    c. I are from China.

2. How old is Roberto?

    a. He am 33 years old.

    b. He are 33 years old.

    c. He is 33 years old.

3. Are they single, married or divorced?

    a. They are married.

    b. They is married.

    c. They am married.

4. Where are Melissa and Henry from?

    a. Melissa are from the United States and Henry are from Korea.

    b. Melissa are from the United States and Henry is from Korea.

    c. Melisa is from the United States and Henry is from Korea.

5. How old are Aaron and Rob?

    a. Aaron is 60 and Rob are 50.

    b. Aaron and Rob are 50.

    c. Aaron and Rob is 60.

F **Use the chart to make up sentences to say to a partner.**

Name	Marital status	Age	Country
Margarita	married	35	Guatemala
Nathan	single	35	United States
Caspar	single	45	Guatemala

EXAMPLE: Margarita and Nathan are 35 years old.

G **Write sentences about you.**

1. (marital status) I _____.

2. (age) I _____.

3. (country) I _____.

Talking with Others

CHALLENGE 2 ➤ Simple Present: *Have/Be*

A Read the identification card.

Felipe   Rodriguez
First name   Last name

8220 State Street
Street address

San Francisco CA 94140
City   State   ZIP

Felipe Rodriguez

B Complete the sentences.

1. The address is _____.

2. The city is _____.

3. The zip code is _____.

4. His first name is _____.

5. His last name is _____.

C Read the charts.

Simple Present: *Have*			
Subject	**Have**	**Information**	**Example sentence**
I, you, we, they	have	black hair	I **have** black hair.
		brown hair	They **have** brown hair.
		blond hair	You **have** blond hair.
he, she, it	has	brown eyes	He **has** brown eyes.
		blue eyes	She **has** blue eyes.

Simple Present: *Be*			
Subject	**Be**	**Information**	**Example sentence**
I	am	5' 6" tall	I **am** 5' 6" tall. (five feet, six inches)
you	are	130 pounds	You **are** 130 pounds.
he, she, it	is	30 years old	She **is** 30 years old.

Simple Present: *Have/Be*

D **Bubble in the correct answers.**

1. John _____ 6' tall.   ○ has   ● is
2. They _____ brown hair.   ○ have   ○ are
3. Margarita and Jan _____ brown eyes.   ○ have   ○ is
4. You _____ 120 pounds.   ○ have   ○ are
5. We _____ blue eyes and blond hair.   ○ have   ○ are
6. I _____ 25 years old   ○ have   ○ am
7. She _____ 5' 5" tall.   ○ has   ○ is
8. I _____ brown hair.   ○ have   ○ am
9. He _____ black hair.   ○ has   ○ is
10. We _____ 32 years old.   ○ have   ○ are

E **Circle the correct answers.**

1. Alfredo (has) / **have** blue eyes.
2. Pauline **has** / **have** brown hair.
3. We **has** / **have** green eyes.
4. Pauline and Alfredo **has** / **have** brown hair.
5. You **has** / **have** blond hair.
6. I **has** / **have** black hair.

7. She **am** / **is** / **are** from Mexico.
8. The teacher **am** / **is** / **are** tall.
9. We **am** / **is** / **are** from Nicaragua.
10. You **am** / **is** / **are** 42 years old.
11. They **am** / **is** / **are** 5' 2" tall.
12. I **am** / **is** / **are** 24 years old.

F **Ask a partner about the people in the pictures.**

Name: Kenji
From: Japan
Marital status: single
Hair: black
Eyes: brown

Name: Anya
From: Russia
Marital status: married
Hair: white
Eyes: blue

Name: Mario
From: Mexico
Marital status: divorced
Hair: black
Eyes: brown

EXAMPLE: *Student A:* Please describe Kenji.
          Student B: He is from Japan. He is single. He has black hair and brown eyes.

G **Write about a partner.**

EXAMPLE: John is from Canada. He is married. He has blond hair and blue eyes.

_____

_____

UNIT **1**

Talking with Others

CHALLENGE 3 ➤ More on Simple Present: *Have/Be*

A Look at the family tree.

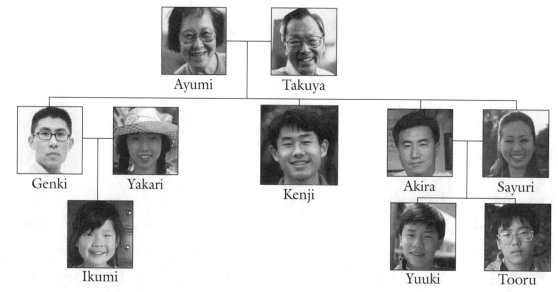

Ayumi   Takuya

Genki   Yakari

Kenji

Akira   Sayuri

Ikumi

Yuuki   Tooru

B Circle the correct answer.

1. Ayumi's husband
   a. Kenji
   b. Ikumi
   c. Takuya

2. Akira's wife
   a. Sayuri
   b. Ayumi
   c. Genki

3. Genki's daughter
   a. Ikumi
   b. Yakari
   c. Takayo

4. Kenji's mother
   a. Sayuri
   b. Ayumi
   c. Takuya

C Read the charts.

Simple Present: *Be*			
Subject	**Be**	**Relationship**	**Example sentence**
he she	is	Roberto's brother Roberto's sister	He **is** Roberto's brother. She **is** Roberto's sister.
they	are	Lien's children Lien's parents	They **are** Lien's children. They **are** Lien's parents.

Simple Present: *Have*			
Subject	**Have**	**Relationship**	**Example sentence**
I, you, we, they	have	brothers sisters	I **have** three brothers. You **have** one sister. We **have** no brothers. They **have** two sisters.
he she	has		He **has** two sisters. She **has** four brothers.

D Complete the sentences with the correct form of *be*.

1. Ayumi _____is_____ Kenji's mother.

2. Yuuki and Tooru _____ Akira's children.

3. Yakari _____ Genki's wife.

4. Akira and Genki _____ Kenji's brothers.

5. I _____ Kenji's sister.

6. We _____ Takuya's children.

E Complete the sentences with *have* or *has*.

1. Kenji _____has_____ two brothers and one sister.

2. Tooru _____ one brother.

3. Yuuki _____ three aunts.

4. Takuya and Ayumi _____ three grandchildren.

5. Ikumi, Yukki, and Tooru _____ six aunts and uncles.

6. We _____ four children.

F Read the paragraphs.

I am Olivia. I am Leonel's daughter. I have three brothers and one sister.

Kenji is single. He is Takuya's son. He has two brothers and one sister.

G Write about you and a partner.

You

I am _____

_____

_____

_____

_____

A Partner

_____

_____

_____

_____

_____

Talking with Others

CHALLENGE 4 ➤ Simple Present: *Like*

A Read the information.

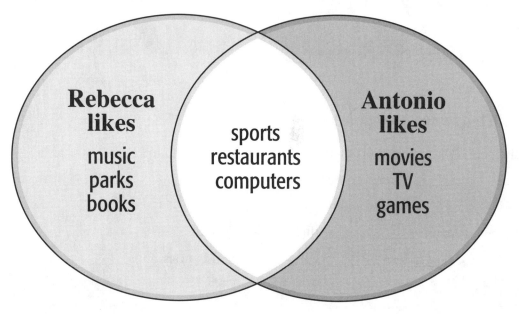

Rebecca likes
music
parks
books

sports
restaurants
computers

Antonio likes
movies
TV
games

B Complete the chart.

Only Rebecca likes . . .	Only Antonio likes . . .	Rebecca and Antonio like . . .

C Read the chart.

Simple Present: *Like*			
Subject	Verb	Information	Example sentence
I	like	movies	I **like** movies.
you			You **like** music.
we		music	We **like** sports.
they		sports	They **like** games.
he	likes	games	He **likes** games.
she		computers	She **likes** computers.

D Circle the correct verb.

1. Amal **like** / **likes** computers.
2. They **like** / **likes** restaurants.
3. We **like** / **likes** school.
4. Maria and Alvin **like** / **likes** parks.
5. I **like** / **likes** books.
6. You **like** / **likes** the teacher.

7. I **like** / **likes** movies.
8. We **like** / **likes** sports.
9. Eva **like** / **likes** restaurants.
10. He **like** / **likes** music.
11. They **like** / **likes** TV.
12. She **like** / **likes** school.

E Complete the paragraph with *like* and *likes*.

Allen is a teacher. Maria is Allen's wife. Allen _____**likes**_____ computers. Maria

_____ restaurants. Maria and Allen _____ parks. Maria reads every

day. She _____ books. Allen listens to the radio every day. He _____

music. They _____ sports, movies, and games. They are happy.

F Complete the chart for Allen and Maria using the information in Exercise E.

Allen likes . . .	Maria likes . . .	Allen and Maria like . . .

G Complete the chart for you and a partner.

I like . . .	My partner likes . . .	We like . . .

Talking with Others

CHALLENGE 5 ➤ Using *from . . . to . . .*

A Read the planner.

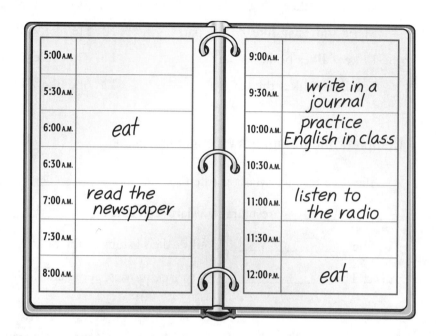

5:00 A.M.	
5:30 A.M.	
6:00 A.M.	*eat*
6:30 A.M.	
7:00 A.M.	*read the newspaper*
7:30 A.M.	
8:00 A.M.	

9:00 A.M.	
9:30 A.M.	*write in a journal*
10:00 A.M.	*practice English in class*
10:30 A.M.	
11:00 A.M.	*listen to the radio*
11:30 A.M.	
12:00 P.M.	*eat*

B Match the clocks to the activities. Write the letter.

    a. listen to the radio   c. read the newspaper

    b. practice English   d. write in a journal

1.   2.   3.   4.

_____   _____   _____

C Read the chart.

Using *from . . . to . . .*				
from	Start time	*to*	End time	Example sentence
	7:00		8:00	He attends school **from** 7:00 **to** 8:00.
from	10:30	to	11:00	He reads **from** 10:30 **to** 11:00.
	5:00		7:00	He practices English **from** 5:00 **to** 7:00.
	8:00		10:00	He watches TV **from** 8:00 **to** 10:00.

D Rewrite the sentences with *from* and *to*.

1. Jerome reads.

   Jerome reads from 7:00 to 8:00.

2. Binh practices English.

   _____

3. Alberto writes in a journal.

   _____

4. Marie listens to the radio.

   _____

5. Hugo watches TV.

   _____

6. Tien reads a newspaper.

   _____

E Read the schedule and write sentences.

Barry's Schedule		
Start	**End**	**Activity**
1. 7:00 A.M.	7:15 A.M.	Barry eats.
2. 9:00 A.M.	10:30 A.M.	Barry practices English.
3. 10:30 A.M.	12:00 P.M.	Barry listens to the radio.

1. Barry eats from 7:00 A.M. to 7:15 A.M. _____

2. _____

3. _____

F When do you practice these things? Write the times. Tell a partner.

1. I practice English _____.

2. I watch TV _____.

3. I listen to the radio _____.

Possessive Adjectives

Talking with Others

EXTENSION CHALLENGE 1 ➤ Possessive Adjectives

A Read the information.

Kenji

Kenji's Schedule

6:00- 7:00	eat
7:00- 8:00	drive to school
8:00-10:00	practice English
10:00-11:00	take a break

Country: Japan
Marital status: single
Hair: black
Eyes: brown
Likes: movies, sports
Family: 2 brothers and 1 sister

B Complete the paragraph about Kenji.

My name is Kenji. I am from _____. I have _____ hair and

_____ eyes. I am _____. I have _____ brothers and

_____ sister. I practice English from _____ to _____.

I like _____ and _____.

C Read the chart.

Possessive Adjectives	
Possession	**Possessive adjectives**
I have a daughter.	**My** daughter has red hair.
You have a brother.	**Your** brother has green eyes.
He has a mother.	**His** mother has new shoes.
She has an aunt.	**Her** aunt is from San Francisco.
We have children.	**Our** children like sports.
They have parents.	**Their** parents are from China.

D Complete the sentences with possessive adjectives.

1. _____My_____ name is Roberto. I have a beautiful family.

2. I have two children. _____ children are happy.

3. My son is 17 years old. _____ name is Juan.

4. My daughter is 15 years old. _____ name is Carla.

5. Juan and Carla both have brown hair. _____ eyes are also brown.

6. My wife Silvia has brown eyes, too. _____ hair is black.

7. I am 45 years old. _____ hair is black and _____ eyes are brown.

8. We all watch TV in the evenings. _____ family is very happy.

E Complete the paragraph with possessive adjectives.

This is a photo of _____my_____ family. This is my daughter. _____ name is

Ana. Ana has two children, Rosalina and Luiz. Both Rosalina and Luiz have the same birthday.

_____ birthday is August 8. Rosalina has blue eyes and _____

hair is red. Luiz has brown eyes and _____ hair is brown. Rosalina likes books.

_____ brother likes sports and movies.

F Complete the sentences about you and a partner. Read your sentences
to your partner and listen to your partner read to you.

_____ name is _____. _____ father's name is

_____. _____ mother's name is _____. We are

from _____. _____ family is _____ (large/small).

My partner's name is _____. _____ father's name is

_____. _____ mother's name is _____. They are

from _____. _____ family is _____ (large/small).

Talking with Others

EXTENSION CHALLENGE 2 ➤ Possessive Proper Nouns

Possessive Proper Nouns

A Look at the family tree.

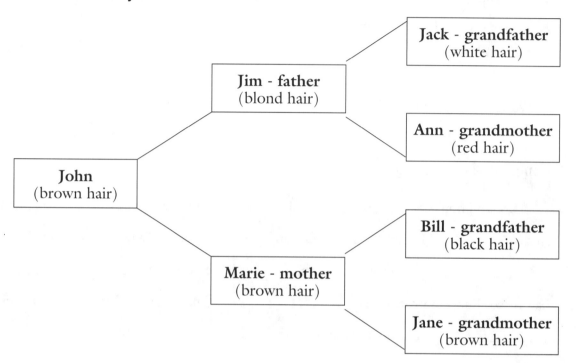

	Jack - grandfather (white hair)
Jim - father (blond hair)	
	Ann - grandmother (red hair)
John (brown hair)	
	Bill - grandfather (black hair)
Marie - mother (brown hair)	
	Jane - grandmother (brown hair)

B Write the names in the chart.

Father	Mother	Grandfather	Grandmother
Jim			

C Read the charts.

Possessive Nouns	
Possession	**Possessive proper nouns**
John has a mother.	**John's** mother has brown hair.
Maria has an aunt.	**Maria's** aunt is from San Francisco.
Michael and David have parents.	**Michael and David's** parents are from China.

Possession	**Possessive proper nouns**
John has a book.	**John's** book is new.
Maria has a pencil.	**Maria's** pencil is yellow.
Michael and David have notebooks.	**Michael and David's** notebooks are green.

Rewrite the sentences with possessive proper nouns.

1. John has a book. It is new.

   <u>John's book is new.</u>

2. Antonio has a sister. She is 24 years old.

   _____

3. Rosalba has a pencil. It is yellow.

   _____

4. Darlene has a friend. She is from Peru.

   _____

5. Lidia has a sister. She has red hair.

   _____

6. Armand has an uncle. He has blue eyes.

   _____

 Write about John's family from Exercise A.

1. Jack

   _____<u>Jack's wife</u>_____ has red hair.

2. Jim

   _____ has white hair.

3. Marie

   _____ has blond hair.

4. John

   _____ has red hair.

5. Jack and Ann

   _____ has brown hair.

6. Marie

   _____ has black hair.

 Talk to a partner about his or her family. Report to the class.

Let's go shopping!

CHALLENGE 1 ➤ Simple Present: *Shop*

Simple Present: *Shop*

A Look at the bar graph.

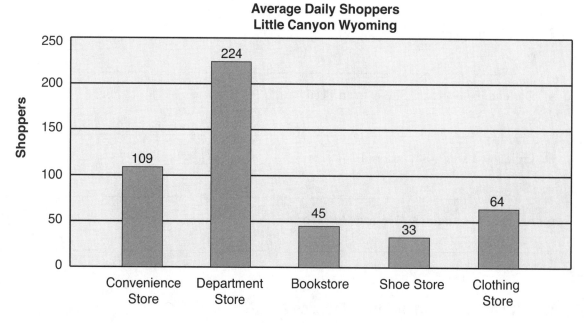

**Average Daily Shoppers
Little Canyon Wyoming**

B Answer the questions about the graph.

1. How many people shop at the bookstore? __45__

2. How many people shop at the shoe store? _____

3. How many people shop at the convenience store? _____

4. How many people shop at the clothing store? _____

5. How many people shop at the department store? _____

C Read the chart.

Simple Present: *Shop*		
Subject	**Verb**	**Example sentence**
I, you, we, they	shop	I **shop** for shoes at a department store.
		You **shop** for bread at a convenience store.
		We **shop** for shorts at a department store.
		They **shop** for books at a bookstore.
he, she, it	shops	He **shops** for shoes at a shoe store.
		She **shops** for dresses at a clothing store.

D Bubble in the correct answers.

1. They _____ for CD players at a department store.   ● shop   ○ shops

2. We _____ for books at the bookstore.   ○ shop   ○ shops

3. I _____ for shirts at a clothing store.   ○ shop   ○ shops

4. Marcos and Renee _____ for food at Sam's Supermarket.   ○ shop   ○ shops

5. Eva _____ for a dress at Cool Breeze Clothing Store.   ○ shop   ○ shops

6. Van and her husband _____ for shoes at a department store.   ○ shop   ○ shops

7. Armand _____ for flowers at the flower shop.   ○ shop   ○ shops

8. Gabriela, Ana, and Paula _____ for clothes every month.   ○ shop   ○ shops

9. You _____ for toys at a toy store.   ○ shop   ○ shops

10. Lidia and I _____ at Ruben's Food and Plenty.   ○ shop   ○ shops

E Read the chart.

Name	Department Store	Convenience Store	Supermarket	Bookstore	Shoe Store	Clothing Store
Richard	shoes, pants	milk, water	groceries	dictionaries		shirts
Alexis	toys		groceries		shoes	shirts

F Complete sentences using the information in Exercise E.

1. Richard __shops for shoes and pants__ at the department store.

2. Alexis _____ at the department store.

3. Richard and Alexis _____ at the supermarket.

4. Alexis _____ at the clothing store.

5. Richard _____ at the bookstore.

6. Richard _____ at the convenience store.

7. Richard and Alexis _____ at the clothing store.

8. Alexis _____ at the department store.

G Ask classmates where they shop.

1. Where do you shop for clothes?   Name: _____   Location: _____

2. Where do you shop for milk?   Name: _____   Location: _____

3. Where do you shop for a paper?   Name: _____   Location: _____

4. Where do you shop for CD's?   Name: _____   Location: _____

Let's go shopping!

CHALLENGE 2 ➤ *How much is/are . . . ?*

A Read the receipt.

MacKay's DEPARTMENT STORE	
Vacuum	$98.99
Washing machine	$450.00
Telephone	$80.00
Toaster	$42.99
Subtotal	$671.98
Tax	$53.76
TOTAL	**$725.74**

B Answer the questions about the receipt.

1. How much is the vacuum cleaner? $ _____
2. How much is the toaster? $ _____
3. How much is the telephone? $ _____
4. What's the tax? $ _____
5. What's the total? $ _____

C Read the chart.

Be Verb (Questions)			
Question words	Be	Nouns	Sample questions
how much (money)	is	the vacuum	How much **is** the vacuum?
		the radio	How much **is** the radio?
how much (money)	are	the shoes	How much **are** the shoes?
		the oranges	How much **are** the oranges?

D Complete the sentences with *are* or *is*.

1. How much _____is_____ the cheese?

2. How much _____ the oranges?

3. How much _____ the shirt?

4. How much _____ the sneakers?

5. How much _____ the hats?

6. How much _____ the book?

7. How much _____ the pencils?

8. How much _____ the pens?

E Write questions for the information below.

1. (radio) _How much is the radio?_

2. (t-shirts) _____?

3. (dictionary) _____?

4. (socks) _____?

5. (shoes) _____?

6. (dress) _____?

7. (bread) _____?

8. (CD player) _____?

F Look at the pictures. Practice with a partner.

two t-shirts	radio	dictionary	socks
$12.99	$45.50	$23.71	$4.99

EXAMPLE: *Student A:* How much are the t-shirts?
          Student B: $12.99.

G In a group, complete the chart for your own department store. Ask: *How much?*

Item	Price
shoes	$18.00

Let's go shopping!

CHALLENGE 3 ➤ *It is, They are*

A Look at the receipt. Fill in the missing numbers.

MacKay's DEPARTMENT STORE	
Baseball cap	$12.99
Blouse	$32.⯑9
Sweater	$4⯑.00
Suit	$2⯑5.4⯑
Tax	$25.⯑7
TOTAL	**$388.40**

B Write the prices.

baseball cap	blouse	sweater	suit

$ __12.99__ $ _____ $ _____ $ _____

C Read the charts.

Be Verb (Questions)			
Question words	**Be**	**Nouns**	**Example question**
how much (money)	is	the dress	How much **is** the dress?
how much (money)	are	the socks	How much **are** the socks?

Be Verb (Answers)		
Subject	**Be**	**Example sentence**
It (the dress, the suit, etc.)	is	It **is** $48. It's $48. (the dress) It **is** $285. It's $285. (the suit)
They (the socks, the ties, etc.)	are	They **are** $12. They're $12. (the socks) They **are** $22. They're $22. (the ties)

Side text: *It is, They are*

D Bubble in the correct answers.

1. (dress) _____ $56.00. ● It is ○ They are
2. (shoes) _____ $28.00. ○ It is ○ They are
3. (skirt) _____ $33.00. ○ It's ○ They're
4. (sweater) _____ $34.99. ○ It is ○ They are
5. (ties) _____ $12.99. ○ It is ○ They are
6. (tennis shoes) _____ $22.50. ○ It's ○ They're
7. (hat) _____ $24. ○ It's ○ They're
8. (t-shirts) _____ $9.99. ○ It's ○ They're

E Write three sentences. Follow the example.

1. shoes / $28.00

The shoes are $28.00.

They are $28.00.

They're $28.00.

2. blouse / $45.00

_____

_____

_____

3. suit / $385.98

_____

_____

_____

4. socks / $15.45

_____

_____

_____

5. tie / $25.55

_____

_____

_____

6. coat / $75.99

_____

_____

_____

F Complete the receipt with information from Exercise D. Tell a partner about the prices.

MacKay's DEPARTMENT STORE	
Shoes	$28.00
TOTAL	

It is, They are

Possessive Adjectives

Let's go shopping!

CHALLENGE 4 ➤ Possessive Adjectives

A Read the descriptions under the pictures.

white blouse
blue slacks
brown shoes
black belt

red shirt
brown shorts
brown sandals
blue cap

B Complete the sentences with information from Exercise A.

1. Gabriela has a _____ blouse.

2. She has _____ slacks.

3. She has _____ shoes.

4. She has a _____ belt.

5. Roberto has a _____ shirt.

6. He has _____ shorts.

7. He has _____ sandals.

8. He has a _____ cap.

C Read the chart.

Possessive Adjectives	
Possession	**Possessive adjectives**
I have a blue shirt.	**My** shirt is blue.
You have a green blouse.	**Your** blouse is green.
He has red shoes.	**His** shoes are red.
She has white pants.	**Her** pants are white.
We have blue hats.	**Our** hats are blue.
They have black shorts.	**Their** shorts are black.

D Write the possessive adjective.

1. They have blue shirts. _____Their_____ shirts are blue.

2. I have red shorts. _____ shorts are red.

3. We have black shoes. _____ shoes are black.

4. You have a white blouse. _____ blouse is white.

5. She has a green coat. _____ coat is green.

6. Anton and I have brown sandals. _____ sandals are brown.

7. Elizabeth and Mario have black pants. _____ pants are black.

8. I have a brown and a black belt. _____ belts are brown and black.

Oscar

red shirt,
blue pants,
black shoes,
black belt

Tom

blue shirt,
blue pants,
black shoes,
brown belt

Catalina

blue blouse,
gray pants
black shoes,
black belt

E Write sentences about Oscar, Tom, and Catalina.

1. Oscar / shirt

   His shirt is red. _____

2. Tom / belt

   _____

3. Catalina / pants

   _____

4. Oscar, Tom, and Catalina / shoes

   _____

5. Oscar, Tom / pants

   _____

6. Catalina / blouse

   _____

Let's go shopping!

CHALLENGE 5 ➤ Adjectives

Adjectives

 A Match the adjective with the picture. Draw a line.

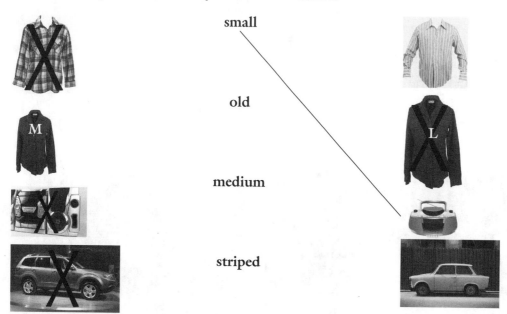

small

old

medium

striped

 B Using the information in Exercise A, complete the following sentences.

1. He wants a small radio and not a _____ radio.

2. He wants an old car and not a _____ car.

3. She wants a medium blouse and not a _____ blouse.

4. He wants a striped shirt and not a _____ shirt.

 C Read the chart.

Adjectives				
Subject	**Verb**	**Adjective**	**Noun**	**Example sentence**
I you we they	want	a big a large a little a small	TV book house	I want a **big** TV. You want a **small** house. We want an **old** book. They want a **used** car.
he she	wants	an old a new a used a medium	blouse car shirt	He wants a **big** shirt. She wants a **medium** blouse. *Note:* Use *a* or *an* with singular count nouns.

D Bubble in the correct answers.

1. I _____ a new car.   ● want   ○ wants

2. The teacher _____ a small radio.   ○ want   ○ wants

3. The students _____ a large TV in the classroom.   ○ want   ○ wants

4. We _____ an old car.   ○ want   ○ wants

5. You _____ a small apartment.   ○ want   ○ wants

6. They _____ an old book from the library.   ○ want   ○ wants

7. I _____ a little dog.   ○ want   ○ wants

8. He _____ a large t-shirt.   ○ want   ○ wants

E Read the descriptions of what Nam, Silvia and Roberto, and Gabriela want.

new house
used car

old house
new car

old house
used car

F Write sentences about Nam, Silvia and Roberto, and Gabriela.

1. Nam <u>wants a new house and a used car</u>.

2. Silvia and Roberto _____.

3. Gabriela _____.

4. Nam and Gabriela _____.

5. Silvia, Roberto, and Gabriela _____.

G What do you want for a house and a car? What does your partner want? Write sentences.

1. I _____.

2. _____.

3. We _____.

Let's go shopping!

EXTENSION CHALLENGE 1 ➤ Singular/Plural

 A Read about Alberta.

My name is Alberta. I am from Guatemala. I live in San Francisco now. I need more clothes. I need a new coat. I need three new dresses. I also need new shoes, maybe one pair. I need a new skirt and three new blouses. I need many things.

B Complete the chart with how many items Alberta needs.

Coat	Dresses	Skirt	Blouses
1			

 C Read the chart.

Singular and Plural			
Regular		Ends in es	
Singular	Plural	Singular	Plural
shirt	shirts	dress	dresses
sock	socks		
coat	coats		
shoe	shoes	Plural only	
blouse	blouses		pants
skirt	skirts		shorts

Mexico

D Write the plurals for the following words.

1. shoe *s* _shoes_
2. suit *s* _suits_
3. radio *s* _radios_
4. dress *es* _dress es_
5. sock *s* _socks_
6. house *s* _houses_
7. car *s* _cars_
8. book *s* _books_

E Complete the paragraph.

My name is Maria. I am from Haiti. I live in West Palm Beach, Florida. I need

more clothes. I need two new _____coats_____ (coat). I need _____

(sandal) and _____ (pant). I need four new _____ (shirt).

I need two _____ (dress) and one _____ (skirt). I also

need a _____ (suit).

F Write a paragraph. What do you need?

> My name is . . . Migue I am From Mexico
>
> I live in Sunnyvale, ca, I need a new
> Shoes a need a socks. also
> need a new car

UNIT **2**

Let's go shopping!

EXTENSION CHALLENGE 2 ➤ Negative Simple Present: Want/Need

A Read the paragraph.

My name is Barry. I live in the United States. I want many things. Some things are very important. I need the important things first.

I want a new house, but I need money first. I want a new car, but I need a used car right now. I need new clothes, I need a new job, and I need a new computer. I want a new $2,000 computer, but I only need a $1,000 computer. It is difficult to know what I need right now and what I want.

B Complete the chart with what Barry wants and needs.

He needs . . .	He wants . . .
money	want a new house
mew ea N	ma ny
erothen	
meNtv conaPutew	

C Read the charts.

Simple Present: *Want/Need*			
Subject	**Verb**	**Noun**	**Example sentence**
I, you, we, they	want	a TV	I **want** a big TV.
	need	a book	You **need** a new book.
he, she	wants	a car	He **wants** a used car.
	needs	a shirt	She **needs** a medium shirt.

Negative Simple Present: *Want/Need*				
Subject	**Negative**	**Verb**	**Noun**	**Example sentences**
I, you, we, they	don't	want	a TV	I **don't want** a big TV.
			a book	You **don't need** a new book.
he, she	doesn't	need	a car	He **doesn't want** a used car.
			a shirt	She **doesn't need** a medium shirt.

D Bubble in the correct answers.

1. I _____ a new car. ● don't want   ○ doesn't want   ○ don't wants
2. We _____ a big radio. ○ don't need   ○ doesn't want   ○ don't wants
3. She _____ a new hat. ○ don't want   ○ doesn't wants   ○ doesn't want
4. They _____a house. ○ don't want   ○ doesn't want   ○ don't needs
5. Tuba _____ a blouse. ○ don't want   ○ doesn't wants   ○ doesn't want
6. I _____ a CD player. ○ don't need   ○ doesn't need   ○ don't needs
7. Molly and Russ _____ a car. ○ don't want   ○ doesn't want   ○ don't wants
8. You _____ shirts. ○ don't need   ○ doesn't wants   ○ doesn't want

E Read the chart.

Armand wants . . .	Armand doesn't want . . .
a large house a new car a big TV	an old house a used car a small TV
Debbie wants . . .	**Debbie doesn't want . . .**
a small house a used car a small TV	an old house a new car a large TV
Armand and Debbie both want . . .	**Armand and Debbie don't want . . .**
a new house a red car a color TV	an old house a black and white TV a computer

F Write sentences about Armand and Debbie.

1. Armand and Debbie both want a new house. _____
2. _____
3. _____
4. _____
5. _____
6. _____

G Complete the chart about you and talk to a partner. Write sentences.

I need . . .	I don't need . . .

UNIT 3 Food

CHALLENGE 1 ➤ Simple Present: *Like*

A Look at the words.

pizza	hamburger	eggs
fried chicken	turkey sandwich	cereal
chicken and rice	spaghetti	roast beef

B Write what you like and what you don't like in the chart.

I like . . .	I don't like . . .

C Read the charts.

Simple Present: *Like*		
Subject	**Verb**	**Example sentence**
I, you, we, they	like	I **like** hamburgers. You **like** french fries. We **like** fried chicken. They **like** roast beef.
he, she, it	likes	He **likes** cereal. She **likes** toast.

Negative Simple Present: *Like*				
Subject	**Negative**	**Verb**	**Noun**	**Example sentence**
I, you, we, they	don't	like	hamburgers	I **don't like** hamburgers.
			french fries	You **don't like** french fries.
he, she	doesn't		fried chicken	He **doesn't like** fried chicken.
			cereal	She **doesn't like** cereal.

D Bubble in the correct words.

1. Dave _likes_ pizza.   ○ don't like   ○ like   ● doesn't like
2. Martha ____ roast beef.   ● likes   ◉ don't like   ○ like
3. Dave and Jane ____ cereal.   ● like   ○ don't likes   ○ doesn't like
4. Ana ____ spaghetti.   ● doesn't like   ○ like   ○ no like
5. We ____ fried chicken.   ● like   ○ likes   ○ doesn't like
6. I ____ French fries.   ● don't like   ○ likes   ○ no like
7. He ____ eggs and toast.   ○ like   ○ don't like   ● doesn't like
8. You ____ peanut butter.   ● like   ○ likes   ○ doesn't like

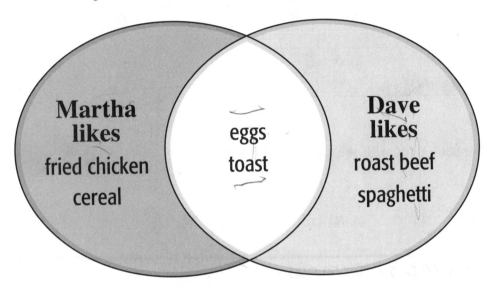

Martha likes fried chicken cereal   eggs toast   **Dave likes** roast beef spaghetti

E Complete the sentences about what Martha and Dave *like* and *don't like*.

1. Martha ___likes___ eggs and fried chicken.
2. Dave _likes_ eggs.
3. Martha _doesnt like_ roast beef.
4. Dave and Martha _like_ toast.
5. Dave _doesnt like_ fried chicken.
6. Dave and Martha _likes_ eggs.

F Write sentences about what you and a partner like.

1. I _like chicken_ .
2. My partner _likes, Red wine_ .
3. We _like, Chicken_ .

Food

CHALLENGE 2 ➤ *How much/How many*

A Look at the containers.

Inventory		
Quantity	**Item**	**Container**
2	milk	gallon
1	spaghetti	package
1	peanut butter	jar
3	soda	six-pack
3	cookies	box
3	potato chips	bag

B Complete the sentences with information in Exercise A.

1. There are _____two gallons_____ of milk.
2. There is _ONe Packag_ of spaghetti.
3. There is _oNe gav_ of peanut butter.
4. There are _TNvec sik-paeles_ of soda.
5. There are _three boxes_ of cookies.
6. There are _three bags_ of potato chips.

C Read the chart.

How much / How many		
	Question	**Answer**
Noncount	**How much** milk is there?	There is one gallon of milk.
Count	**How many** gallons of milk are there?	There are two gallons of milk.
	How many avocados are there?	There are three avocados.

Question words	Verb	Nouns	Example question
how much (money)	is	the milk	How much **is** the milk?
how much (money)	are	the tomatoes	How much **are** the tomatoes?

How much/How many

D) Write *How many* or *How much*.

1. _____How many_____ gallons of milk are there?
2. _____How many_____ jars of mustard are there?
3. _____How much_____ yogurt is there?
4. _____How many_____ bags of potato chips are there?
5. _____How much_____ is the spaghetti?
6. _____How many_____ avocados are there?
7. _____How many_____ packages of spaghetti are there?
8. _____How much_____ are the tomatoes?
9. _____How much_____ ground beef is there?
10. _____How much_____ water is there?

E) Write *how much is* or *how much are*.

1. _____How much are_____ the avocados?
2. _____ the butter?
3. _____ the oranges?
4. _____ the carrots?
5. _____ the ground beef?
6. _____ the milk?
7. _____ the sugar?
8. _____ the cookies?
9. _____ the peanut butter?
10. _____ the potato chips?
11. _____ the spaghetti?
12. _____ the tomatoes?

F) Ask a partner what is in his or her house. Fill in the chart.

EXAMPLE: *Student A:* How many gallons of milk are there in your house?
Student B: There are three gallons.

Inventory		
Quantity	**Item**	**Container**
	milk	gallon
	spaghetti	package
	peanut butter	jar
	soda	six-pack
	cookies	box
	potato chips	bag

CHALLENGE 3 ➤ Simple Present

Simple Present *(side tab)*

A Look at the shopping list.

Shopping List
3 jars of peanut butter
2 cans of soup
2 bottles of oil
3 packages of spaghetti
3 cans of tomato sauce

B Practice the conversation with a partner. Ask about the shopping list in Exercise A.

Roberto: What do we need at the store?
Eva: We need soup.
Roberto: How much do we need?
Eva: We need two cans.

C Read the chart.

Simple Present		
Subject	**Verb**	**Example sentence**
I, you, we, they	eat	I **eat** tacos for lunch.
	like	You **like** eggs for breakfast.
	need	We **need** three cans of corn.
	want	They **want** three boxes of cookies.
	make	I **make** sandwiches for lunch.
he, she, it	eats	He **eats** pizza for dinner.
	likes	She **likes** tomato soup.
	needs	He **needs** three pounds of tomatoes.
	wants	She **wants** two bottles of water.
	makes	She **makes** sandwiches for Duong.

D Write the correct form of the verbs.

1. She _____eats_____ (eat) roast beef sandwiches.
2. They _____ (like) a big breakfast.
3. We _____ (need) two gallons of water.
4. Vinicio and Laura _____ (want) tuna fish sandwiches.
5. I _____ (make) a turkey sandwich every day for lunch.
6. The students _____ (eat) pizza every week.
7. He _____ (like) tomatoes on his hamburger.
8. Hugo and I _____ (need) water and soda.
9. Pablo _____ (eat) lunch at noon.
10. Minh _____ (make) sandwiches for Duong.

E Look at the charts.

Duong Sandwiches	like	eat	make
turkey	X	X	
tuna fish		X	
roast beef	X	X	
peanut butter	X	X	X

Minh Sandwiches	like	eat	make
turkey	X	X	X
tuna fish	X	X	X
roast beef	X		
peanut butter			X

F Complete the sentences with the correct form of the verbs. Look at Exercise E.

1. Minh _____makes_____ turkey, tuna fish, and peanut butter sandwiches.
2. Duong doesn't like tuna fish, but he _____ tuna fish.
3. Duong _____ turkey, tuna fish, roast beef, and peanut butter sandwiches.
4. Duong and Minh _____ tuna fish sandwiches.
5. Minh _____ roast beef sandwiches.
6. Duong and Minh _____ roast beef sandwiches.

G Complete the charts about you and your partner. Then, report to a group.

You Sandwiches	like	eat	make
turkey			
tuna fish			
roast beef			
peanut butter			

Your Partner Sandwiches	like	eat	make

Food

CHALLENGE 4 ➤ Comparative Adjectives

Comparative Adjectives

A Read the chart.

Food	Van's Supermarket	Albert's Supermarket
bananas	$1.25 a pound	$1.35 a pound
oil	$3.00 a bottle	$2.75 a bottle
tuna	$ .99 a can	$ .96 a can
cereal	$3.69 a box	$3.99 a box
jelly	$2.10 a jar	$2.25 a jar

B Answer the questions with the information in Exercise A.

1. How much are the bananas at Albert's? <u>$1.35 a pound</u>

2. How much is the jelly at Van's? _____

3. How much is one box of cereal plus one can of tuna at Van's? _____

4. How much is a bottle of oil plus a pound of bananas at Albert's? _____

5. How much is one bottle of oil plus a pound of bananas at Van's? _____

6. How much is a jar of jelly at Albert's? _____

C Read the chart.

Comparative Adjectives		
	Question	**Answer**
Singular	Where is ground beef cheaper?	It's cheaper at Puente Market.
Plural	Where are carrots cheaper?	They're cheaper at Food City.
	Question	**Answer**
Singular	Where is ground beef more expensive?	It's more expensive at Puente Market.
Plural	Where are carrots more expensive?	They're more expensive at Food City.

D Look at Exercise A. Complete the sentences with *cheaper* or *more expensive*.

1. Bananas are _____ cheaper _____ at Van's.

2. Oil is _____ at Albert's.

3. Cereal is _____ at Albert's.

4. Tuna is _____ at Albert's.

5. Jelly is _____ at Albert's.

6. Oil is _____ at Van's.

E Look at Exercise A. Write the name of the store.

1. Jelly is cheaper at _____ Van's Supermarket _____.

2. Tuna is more expensive at _____.

3. Bananas are more expensive at _____.

4. Oil is cheaper at _____.

5. Cereal is cheaper at _____.

6. Bananas are cheaper at _____.

F Answer the questions with complete sentences.

1. Where are bananas cheaper?

   They're cheaper at Van's. _____

2. Where is tuna more expensive?

   _____

3. Where is oil cheaper?

   _____

4. Where is cereal more expensive?

   _____

5. Where is jelly cheaper?

   _____

G Write good prices and compare with a partner.

My Store	My Partner's Store
apples: $_____	apples: $_____
sugar: $_____	sugar: $_____
carrots: $_____	carrots: $_____

Comparative Adjectives

Food

CHALLENGE 5 ➤ Short Answers

(A) Read the order.

Order

TABLE NO. 4	SERVER NO. Marilyn

1 roast beef sandwich	$ 2.99
1 order of french fries	$ 1.49
1 soda	$ .99
1 ice cream	$ 1.29
Tax	$ .54
TOTAL	$ 7.30

(B) Answer the questions with short answers.

1. How much is the tax? _____It's 54 cents._____

2. How much is the total? _____

3. How much is the drink? _____

4. How much is the sandwich? _____

5. Does he want ice cream? _____

6. Does he want milk? _____

(C) Read the chart.

Short Answers		
Question	**Yes**	**No**
Do you want a hamburger?	Yes, I do.	No, I don't. Thank you.
Do they want sandwiches?	Yes, they do.	No, they don't.
Does he want a sandwich?	Yes, he does.	No, he doesn't.
Does she want a sandwich?	Yes, she does.	No, she doesn't.

D **Look at what the students want to eat.**

Name	Turkey sandwich	Soda	French fries	Chocolate ice cream
Sebastien	yes	yes	yes	yes
Ana	no	no	no	yes
Andre	yes	no	no	no
Kim	yes	no	yes	yes

 E **Answer the questions. Use short answers.**

1. Does Ana want ice cream? _____Yes, she does._____

2. Does Andre want a soda? _____

3. Do Andre and Ana want french fries? _____

4. Does Sebastien want a sandwich and french fries? _____

5. Does Kim want a soda? _____

6. Does Kim want a sandwich? _____

7. Do Sebastien and Kim want ice cream? _____

8. Does Ana want a sandwich? _____

 F **Read the chart and practice the conversation with a partner.**

	Turkey sandwich	Soda	French fries	Chocolate ice cream
Number 1	yes	yes	no	yes
Number 2	yes	no	yes	yes
Number 3	no	yes	yes	yes
Number 4	yes	yes	yes	no

EXAMPLE: Number 1

Student A: Can I take your order?
Student B: Yes. I want a turkey sandwich and a soda.
Student A: Do you want french fries?
Student B: No, I don't. Thank you.
Student A: Do you want dessert?
Student B: Yes, I do. I want chocolate ice cream.
Student A: OK.

G **Write your own conversation and present it to the class.**

Food

EXTENSION CHALLENGE 1 ➤ Comparing Nouns

A Read the sign over the highway fruit stand.

B Answer the questions with the information in Exercise A.

1. Bita bought 2 pounds of apples. She spent ___$4___.

2. Miyuki bought a dozen limes. She spent _____.

3. Juan bought a dozen lemons. He spent _____.

4. Charity bought a pound of bananas, a papaya and a mango. She spent _____.

5. Morteza bought a pound of grapes and a pound of bananas. He spent _____.

6. Lam bought 10 oranges. They weighed 1½ pounds. He spent _____.

7. Hilda bought 3 pounds of tomatoes. She spent _____.

8. Lilia bought a papaya and Courtney bought a mango. They spent _____.

C Read the chart.

Comparing Nouns				
Subject	**Be**	**Comparative adjective**	**Noun**	**Example sentence**
milk	is	cheaper than	juice	Milk is **cheaper than** juice.
apples	are	cheaper than	bananas	Apples are **cheaper than** bananas.
Subject	**Be**	**Comparative adjective**	**Noun**	**Example sentence**
juice	is	more expensive than	milk	Juice is **more expensive than** milk.
bananas	are	more expensive than	apples	Bananas are **more expensive than** apples.

D Look at the chart again in Exercise A. Complete the sentences.

1. By the pound, apples are _____cheaper than_____ oranges.

2. A dozen lemons are _____ a dozen limes.

3. An avocado is _____ a papaya.

4. Three pounds of tomatoes _____ one pound of oranges.

5. A pound of grapes is _____ 4 pounds of bananas.

6. A mango is _____ an avocado.

7. Five pounds of bananas are _____ one pound of apples.

8. Five pounds of bananas are _____ one pound of oranges.

E Using the information in Exercise A, put the fruits in the chart from cheaper to more expensive by the pound.

apples	tomatoes	bananas	oranges	grapes

cheaper ————————————————————————→ more expensive

bananas				

F Read the chart below. Circle *True* or *False.*

cheaper ————————————————————————→ more expensive

beans	bread	orange juice	sugar	ground beef

1. The orange juice is cheaper than the sugar	(True)	False
2. The bread is more expensive than the sugar.	True	False
3. The beans are more expensive than the sugar.	True	False
4. The ground beef is cheaper than the bread.	True	False
5. The orange juice is more expensive than the beans.	True	False
6. The ground beef is more expensive than the beans.	True	False
7. The orange juice is more expensive than the ground beef.	True	False
8. The bread is cheaper than the orange juice.	True	False

G Look at Exercise A again. In a group, talk about the fruits you like. Say what is cheaper and more expensive.

EXAMPLE: I like bananas. They are cheaper than oranges.

Negative Simple Present

EXTENSION CHALLENGE 2 ➤ Negative Simple Present

A Read the menu.

MARIO'S *Sandwich Shop*

SALADS		SANDWICHES	
Fresh green salad	$1.85	Tuna	$2.50
Caesar salad	$2.50	Roast beef	$2.75
Chicken salad	$2.75	Ham	$2.50
		Turkey	$2.50
BEVERAGES		Cheese	$2.25
Coffee	$1.00	SIDE ORDERS	
Milk	$1.25	Potato chips	$ .89
Soda	$2.00	French fries	$1.19

B Write your order for lunch.

MARIO'S *Order* Sandwich Shop	
TOTAL	

C Read the chart.

Negative Simple Present			
Subject	Negative	Verb	Example sentences
I, you, we, they	don't	eat like	I **don't** eat bananas. You **don't** like peanut butter.
he, she	doesn't	need want	He **doesn't** need apples. She **doesn't** want ice cream.

Circle *don't* or *doesn't*.

1. John **don't** / **doesn't** like turkey sandwiches.
2. I **don't** / **doesn't** eat turkey.
3. She **don't** / **doesn't** make salad.
4. We **don't** / **doesn't** need money for lunch.
5. Tim and Karen **don't** / **doesn't** want breakfast.
6. Alton **don't** / **doesn't** like the sandwiches.
7. Jessica and I **don't** / **doesn't** need the menu.
8. They **don't** / **doesn't** make hamburgers here.
9. You **don't** / **doesn't** eat Caesar salads.
10. I **don't** / **doesn't** make coffee.

E **Complete the sentences with the negative form of the verbs in parentheses.**

1. Matilda and Lonnie _____don't like_____ (like) restaurants.
2. I _____ (eat) fish.
3. We _____ (make) sandwiches.
4. They _____ (serve) pie.
5. He _____ (work) at the restaurant.
6. She _____ (eat) beef.
7. You _____ (drive) to the supermarket.
8. They _____ (go) to the supermarket on Sunday.
9. I _____ (see) the hamburgers on the menu.
10. She _____ (drink) coffee.

F **Complete the sentences about you and your partner.**

1. I don't eat _____.
2. I don't like _____.
3. I don't make _____.
4. I don't need _____.
5. I don't want _____.

1. My partner doesn't eat _____.
2. My partner doesn't like _____.
3. My partner doesn't make _____.
4. My partner doesn't need _____.
5. My partner doesn't want _____.

UNIT **4**

Housing

CHALLENGE 1 ➤ Simple Present: *Live* and Prepositions

 A **Read the paragraph.**

Kenji is from Japan. He lives in an apartment in Newel, Indiana. He lives at 77362 West Park Place. His parents, brothers, and sister live in Japan. Kenji lives with his uncle and aunt. He works around the corner from the apartment at a restaurant.

B **Answer the questions about Kenji. Use short answers.**

1. Does Kenji live in an apartment, a house, or a condominium? _____ An apartment. _____

2. Where is he from? _____

3. Where does his family live? _____

4. Who does he live with? _____

5. Where does he work? _____

C **Read the chart.**

Simple Present: *Live* and Prepositions			
Subject	**Verb**	**Preposition**	**Example sentence**
I, you, we, they	live	in at on	I live **in** a house. You live **at** 4220 Greenburg St. We live **in** Miami. They live **on** First St.
he, she, it	lives	with	He lives **with** his wife. She lives **in** an apartment.

D Complete the sentences with *live* or *lives*.

1. She _____lives_____ in an apartment.
2. They _____ in a house.
3. Kenji's parents _____ in a house.
4. They _____ in Osaka, Japan.
5. You _____ at 3750 Main St.
6. The beautiful woman _____ in Texas.
7. We _____ at 1313 Whitaker St.

8. The children _____ nearby.
9. They _____ in a condominium.
10. He _____ with his parents.
11. She _____ with her friends.
12. They _____ in Pittsburg.
13. The man _____ on Second St.
14. You _____ in a house.

 E Look at the information.

Tren

___Tren Hong___

Address: 1711 Pederson Dr.
City: Victorville
State: California
Housing: house
Marital status: married

Duong

___Duong Bui___

Address: 221 Eastmond Lane
City: New York City
State: New York
Housing: apartment
Marital status: divorced

Alan

___Alan Hart___

Address: 1919 Goldenwest St.
City: Palmdale
State: California
Housing: apartment
Marital status: divorced

 F Complete the sentences with information from Exercise E.

1. Tren _____lives_____ ___in___ a house.
2. Duong _____ _____ 221 Eastmond Lane.
3. Alan _____ _____ Goldenwest St.
4. Duong _____ _____ New York.
5. Duong and Alan _____ _____ apartments.
6. Tren and Alan _____ _____ California.
7. Tren _____ _____ her husband.
8. Alan _____ _____ 1919 Goldenwest St.

 G Ask a partner where he lives and report to a group.

EXAMPLE: *Student A:* Where do you live?
            Student B: I live in a house in Corbin at 13 Main Street.

CHALLENGE 2 ➤ Simple Present: *Have/Has*

A **Look at the floor plan.**

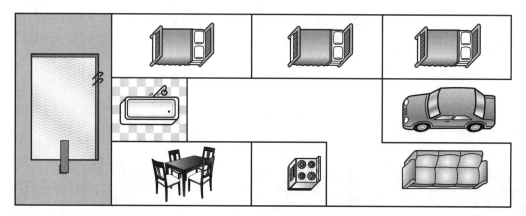

B **Answer the questions.**

1. How many bedrooms are there? _____three bedrooms_____

2. How many bathrooms are there? _____

3. Is there a kitchen? _____

4. Is there a garage? _____

5. Is there a dining room? _____

6. Is there a swimming pool? _____

C **Read the chart.**

Simple Present: *Have*		
Subject	**Have**	**Example sentence**
I, you, we, they	have	I **have** a two-bedroom house. You **have** a big house. We **have** a small kitchen. They **have** a small yard.
he, she, it	has	He **has** a new condominium. She **has** a balcony. It **has** a swimming pool.

D Complete the sentences with *have* or *has*.

1. The condominium _____has_____ a balcony.
2. It _____ a large backyard.
3. Melissa _____ an old house.
4. Margie and Alex _____ a pool.
5. We _____ a big kitchen.
6. The house _____ a large garage.

7. He _____ a beautiful house.
8. They _____ a small apartment.
9. You _____ a front porch.
10. It _____ three bedrooms.
11. We _____ a new condominium.
12. I _____ a big kitchen.

E Look at the information.

Apartment for Rent	**Condominium for Sale**	**House for Sale**
3 bedrooms, 2 bathrooms, near schools. Call: 555-3367.	3 bedrooms, 1 bathroom, pool. Call: 555-2456.	2 bedrooms, 2 bathrooms, big kitchen, two-car garage, pool. Call: 555-6789.

F Complete the sentences about Exercise E.

1. The house _____has_____ two bedrooms.
2. The apartment and the house _____ two bathrooms.
3. The condominium and the apartment _____ three bedrooms.
4. The condominium _____ one bathroom.
5. The house _____ a two-car garage.
6. The condominium and the house _____ a pool.
7. The house _____ a big kitchen.
8. The apartment _____ two bathrooms.

G Check (✓) what your home has. Tell a group.

____ garage
____ kitchen
____ bedroom
____ back yard

____ swimming pool
____ hall
____ deck
____ driveway

____ bathroom
____ balcony
____ stairs

____ family room
____ front porch
____ front yard

Housing

CHALLENGE 3 ➤ *Yes/No* Questions

A Read the advertisements for apartments a, b, c, and d.

a.
3 bed, 2 bath apt.
a/c, balcony,
$800.
Call Lien at
555-7744.

b.
$770 a month.
1 bed, 1 bath apt.
n/pets.
Call Fred at
555-7164.

c.
2 bed, 3 bath hse.
a/c, elect. pd.
Call Margaret for
more information
555-5678.

d.
3 bed, 3 bath
apt. w/pool,
utls pd,
nr schools.
Call 555-5987.

B Write the abbreviations.

Word	Abbreviation
air-conditioning	a/c
apartment	
bathroom	
bedroom	
electricity	
near	
paid	
utilities	
with	

C Read the chart.

Yes/No Questions	
Question	Short answers
Does it have three bedrooms?	Yes, it does. No, it doesn't.
Does it have air-conditioning?	Yes, it does. No, it doesn't.
Do they have three bathrooms?	Yes, they do. No, they don't.

Yes/No Questions

D Answer the questions about Exercise A. Use short answers.

1. Does apartment "a" have a balcony? _____Yes, it does._____

2. Does apartment "a" have air-conditioning? _____

3. Does apartment "d" have air-conditioning? _____

4. Do apartments "c" and "d" have three bathrooms? _____

5. Do apartments "a" and "c" have one bathroom? _____

6. Does apartment "d" have a pool? _____

7. Does apartment "b" have a pool? _____

8. Do apartments "b" and "d" have air-conditioning? _____

E Practice the conversation.

Renter: Excuse me. I need a house to rent.
Agent: We have a three-bedroom house on Sycamore Street.
Renter: Does it have a backyard?
Agent: Yes, it does.
Renter: Does it have a pool?
Agent: No, it doesn't.

F Here is some information about a different house. Read the information.

✓ a garage	___ a swimming pool	✓ front porch	✓ family room
✓ a big kitchen	✓ backyard	___ balcony	___ front yard
✓ three bedrooms	✓ two bathrooms	___ stairs	___ laundry room

G Repeat the conversation in Exercise E, but use the new information from Exercise F.

H Ask a friend *Yes/No* questions about his or her home. Write an "X" for *yes* answers.

___ garage	___ swimming pool	___ bathroom	___ family room
___ kitchen	___ hall	___ balcony	___ front porch
___ bedroom	___ deck	___ stairs	___ front yard
___ backyard	___ driveway	___ laundry room	___ backyard

UNIT **Housing**

CHALLENGE 4 ➤ Present Continuous

 Practice the conversation.

Owner: Hello.
Felipe: Hello. My name is Felipe. <u>I'm calling</u> about the apartment you have for rent.
Owner: Yes. It is available.
Felipe: When can I see it?
Owner: What are you doing right now?
Felipe: Right now, <u>I'm working</u>.
Owner: Oh, can you come on Saturday?
Felipe: I think so.
Owner: The apartment is beautiful. <u>I'm cleaning</u> it right now.
Felipe: OK. I will see you on Saturday.
Owner: OK. Goodbye.

 Circle the correct answer to each question.

1. What are Felipe and the owner doing?
   a. They are talking.
   b. They are eating.
   c. They are looking at an apartment.
2. Why is Felipe calling?
   a. He is a friend.
   b. He is looking for an apartment.
   c. He is cleaning an apartment.
3. What is the owner doing?
   a. She is talking and eating.
   b. She is talking and cleaning.
   c. She is looking for an apartment.

C **Read the chart.**

Present Continuous			
Subject	*Be*	**Base verb + *ing***	**Example sentence**
I	am	talk + *ing*	I **am talking** on the phone.
you, we, they	are	read + *ing* call + *ing*	We **are calling** for an appointment.
he, she, it	is	look + *ing* at look + *ing* for move + *ing*	She **is moving** into a new apartment.

D Write the verbs in the present continuous.

1. Luis and Chen _____ are looking _____ (look) for an apartment to rent.

2. Herman _____ (call) for information about a house for sale.

3. Natalia and Rickie _____ (read) the newspaper.

4. I _____ (move) to a new apartment soon.

5. Karen and I _____ (talk) on the phone about a house on Main Street.

6. They _____ (clean) the apartment.

7. He _____ (paint) the apartment blue.

8. You _____ (talk) to the manager.

E Rewrite the sentences in the present continuous.

1. The owner sells the house for $250,000.

   The owner is selling the house for $250,000.

2. We call for information about an apartment.

   _____

3. They read the classified ads.

   _____

4. We look for a home on Sycamore Street.

   _____

F Eva, Alex, and Franco are working in their house. Look at what they are doing. Write sentences using the present continuous.

To-Do List			
Name	paint	sweep	mop
Eva	x	x	
Alex			x
Franco	x	x	x

1. Eva and Franco _____.

2. Alex _____.

3. Alex and Franco _____.

4. Eva _____.

Housing

CHALLENGE 5 ➤ Prepositions

Prepositions

A Match the pictures with the room. Draw a line.

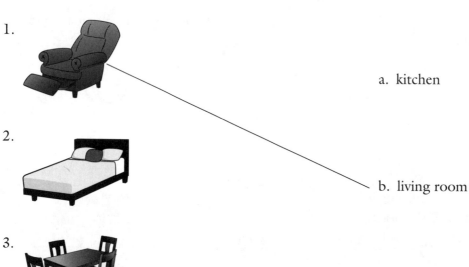

1.

2.

3.

4.

5.

a. kitchen

b. living room

c. bedroom

d. dining room

e. garage

B Circle *True* or *False*.

1. The bed is in the living room.	True	(False)
2. The refrigerator is in the kitchen.	True	False
3. The car is in the garage.	True	False
4. The dining room set is in the kitchen.	True	False
5. The recliner chair is in the living room.	True	False

Prepositions			
The ball is **in** the box.		The ball is **between** two boxes.	
The ball is **on** the box.		The ball is **over** the box.	
The ball is **under** the box.		The ball is **in front of** the box.	
The ball is **next to** the box.		The ball is **behind** the box.	

- Use prepositions to talk about where things are.

C **Look at the pictures in the chart above and write sentences.**

1. the coffee table the sofa

   The coffee table is in front of the sofa.

2. the lamp the table

   _____

3. the bed the tables

   _____

4. the refrigerator the oven

   _____

5. the picture the recliner

   _____

6. the cat the dining room table

   _____

D **Write sentences about the furniture and other things in the classroom.**

1. (between) _____

2. (in back of) _____

3. (next to) _____

4. (under) _____

5. (over) _____

6. (in) _____

UNIT 4 **Housing**

EXTENSION CHALLENGE 1 ➤ Negative Simple Present: *Be*

A Read the paragraph.

Katrina and John live in a house on Ball Road. They have a nice family. They are moving to a new house. The new house has a kitchen, three bedrooms, and two bathrooms. It isn't near schools. It has a balcony. There isn't a garage, a swimming pool, or a front yard, but there is a fenced-in backyard. They like the neighborhood.

B Complete the list about Katrina and John's new house.

There is . . .	There isn't . . .
a kitchen	

C Read the chart.

Negative Simple Present: *Be*			
Subject	**Verb**	**Negative**	**Example sentence (Contractions)**
I	am		I **am not** in the garage. (**I'm not**)
you, we, they	are	not	You **are not** outside. (You're not) (You **aren't**)
			We **are not** outside. (We're not) (We **aren't**)
			They **are not** in the kitchen. (They're not) (They **aren't**)
he, she, it	is		He **is not** in the apartment. (He's not) (He **isn't**)
			She **is not** in the apartment. (She's not) (She **isn't**)
			It **is not** in the living room. (It's not) (It **isn't**)
	Verb	**Negative**	**Example sentence (Contractions)**
There	is	not	There **is not** a front yard. (There **isn't**)
There	are		There **are not** any flowers in the backyard. (There **aren't**)

Rewrite the sentences with contractions.

1. They are not on the front porch. They are in the backyard.
   <u>They're not on the front porch. They're in the backyard.</u>

2. It is in a good neighborhood. It is not a bad neighborhood.

   _____

3. We are not from San Francisco. We are from Dallas.

   _____

4. She is not outside. She is inside.

   _____

5. There is not a deck. There is a large backyard.

   _____

6. They are not in the house. They are in the garage.

   _____

 Read the information.

Furniture	chairs	dresser	bed	sofa	refrigerator
kitchen					X
dining room	X				
bedroom	X	X	X		
living room	X			X	

 Answer the questions about the chart in Exercise E. Write complete sentences.

1. Are there chairs in the living room?
   <u>Yes, there are chairs in the living room.</u>

2. Is there a dresser in the kitchen?

   _____

3. Is there a bed in the living room?

   _____

4. Are there chairs in the bedroom?

   _____

EXTENSION CHALLENGE 2 ➤ Negative Present Continuous

Negative Present Continuous

A Read the paragraph.

Kevin and his family are selling their house. They need to do many things to get it ready. Kevin cleans, paints, and cooks when everyone is hungry. Paul paints and repairs. He doesn't clean. David cleans. Carla paints and repairs things. She doesn't cook and she doesn't clean. Kim cooks, repairs, and cleans. She doesn't paint.

B Complete the chart using the information from Exercise A.

To-Do List				
Name	paint	clean	repair	cook
Kevin	X			
Paul				
David				
Carla				
Kim				

C Read the chart.

Negative Present Continuous				
Subject	Be		Base verb + *ing*	Example sentences
I	am		talk + *ing*	I **am not talking** on the phone.
you, we, they	are	not	read + *ing* call + *ing*	We **are not calling** for an appointment.
he, she, it	is		look + *ing* at look + *ing* for move + *ing*	She **is not moving** into a new apartment.

D Bubble in the correct answers.

1. They _____ cleaning the kitchen.   ○ isn't   ● aren't   ○ am not
2. I _____ repairing the sink.   ○ isn't   ○ aren't   ○ am not
3. She _____ cooking dinner.   ○ isn't   ○ aren't   ○ am not
4. We _____ painting the living room.   ○ isn't   ○ aren't   ○ am not
5. David _____ working on the house.   ○ isn't   ○ aren't   ○ am not
6. You _____ selling this house!   ○ isn't   ○ aren't   ○ am not
7. Harold _____ talking to the agent.   ○ isn't   ○ aren't   ○ am not
8. I _____ calling for an appointment.   ○ isn't   ○ aren't   ○ am not
9. They _____ looking for a new home.   ○ isn't   ○ aren't   ○ am not
10. We _____ moving soon.   ○ isn't   ○ aren't   ○ am not

E Write the negative present continuous.

1. Kevin _____ isn't repairing _____ (repair) the furniture.
2. Paul _____ (clean) the backyard.
3. David _____ (paint) the bedroom.
4. David and Carla _____ (cook) dinner for the family.
5. Paul and Carla _____ (clean) the living room.
6. Kim and I _____ (paint) the bathroom.
7. We _____ (work) on the house.
8. I _____ (talk) to the renter.

F Complete the paragraph. Use only the negative present continuous.

John and his family are selling their house. They need to do many things to get it ready. They need to clean, repair, and paint. John _____ isn't cleaning _____ (clean) right now because he is working in the kitchen with his wife. His daughter is Lydia. She _____ (clean) her room because she is watching TV. Ned _____ (paint) his room because he is cleaning it first. Marjorie is John's wife. She _____ (work) on the house because she is making everyone dinner and John is helping. They _____ (work) very fast. After dinner, they will work on the house.

Our Community

CHALLENGE 1 ➤ *Need to*

A Match the location with the problem. Draw a line.

1.

2.

3.

4.

a. I need to learn English.

b. I need to send a package.

c. There is an emergency.

d. I need to relax.

B Write four places you might find in a city.

_____hotel_____   _____

_____   _____

C Read the chart.

Need to			
Subject	***Need***	**Infinitive**	**Example sentence**
I, you, we, they	need	to go	I **need to go** to the hospital.
		to drive	You **need to drive** to the store.
		to send	We **need to send** a letter.
		to see	They **need to see** the doctor.
he, she, it	needs	to buy	He **needs to buy** a book.
		to look for	She **needs to look for** a house.

Circle *need* or *needs*.

1. Ruby **need** / **needs** to work in the factory on Friday to pay the rent.
2. They **need** / **needs** to go to the real estate agent to find a house.
3. Antonio **need** / **needs** to visit the DMV to get a license.
4. We **need** / **needs** to find a hotel to sleep tonight.
5. I **need** / **needs** to go to the dentist's office to have an examination.
6. She **need** / **needs** to go to school to learn English.

 Look at the sentences in Exercise D. Answer the questions.

1. Why does Ruby need to work?

   To pay the rent.

2. Why do they need to go to the real estate office?

   _____

3. Why does Antonio need to visit the DMV?

   _____

4. Why do we need to find a hotel?

   _____

5. Why do you need to go to the dentist?

   _____

6. Why does she need to go to school?

   _____

F **Use *need* or *needs* and the words in the box to complete the sentences.**

go to the hospital	drive to the park	send a letter	see a police officer
buy a new car	look for a new house	talk to the doctor	eat lunch

1. She is very sick. She ___needs to go to the hospital___.
2. They live in an apartment. They _____.
3. Marco is at the post office. He _____.
4. He has a driver's license but no car. He _____.
5. We are hungry. Let's find a good restaurant. We _____.
6. You are going to Doctor Smith's office. You _____.
7. You lost your purse. You _____.
8. The park is five miles from here. I _____.

 Tell a group where you need to go after school today and this week.

Our Community

CHALLENGE 2 ➤ Imperatives

A Look at the map.

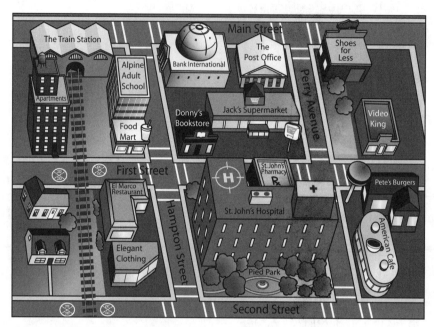

B Complete the sentences about the map above.

1. The train station is on _____Main_____ Street.

2. St. John's Hospital is on _____ Street.

3. Elegant Clothing is on the corner of _____ and _____.

4. Food Mart is on _____ Street.

C Read the chart.

Imperatives			
Subject	**Verb**		**Example sentence**
~~you~~	turn	left	**Turn** left.
~~you~~	turn	right	**Turn** right.
~~you~~	turn	around	**Turn** around.
~~you~~	go	straight ahead	**Go** straight ahead.
~~you~~	stop		**Stop!**
~~you~~	make	a U-turn	**Make** a U-turn.
Example: Go straight ahead. Turn left at First Street. Turn right on Main Street. Stop.			

D Bubble in the correct verb in the imperative.

1. ____ left on First Street. ○ Turns ● Turn ○ He turns
2. ____ on the left. ○ Stop ○ Stops ○ Is stopping
3. ____ straight ahead. ○ Going ○ goes ○ Go
4. ____ around. ○ Stop ○ Turns ○ Turn
5. ____ right at the intersection. ○ Is turning ○ Going ○ Turn
6. ____! ○ Goes ○ Turning ○ Stop

E Add periods and capital letters to the directions.

1. turn around go straight ahead three miles turn left on Mulberry Avenue turn right on Prentice Street sop on the left

   <u>Turn around. Go Straight ahead three miles. Turn left on Mulberry Avenue. Turn right on Prentice Street. Stop on the left.</u>

2. go straight ahead to Montgomery Street turn left on Main stop on the left

   _____

   _____

3. turn left on fifth Avenue turn right on Kennedy Street stop straight ahead

   _____

   _____

4. make a u-turn turn on Adams go straight ahead three blocks stop on the right

   _____

   _____

5. turn right on Jacob's Place make a u-turn at the light turn left on Pine stop

   _____

   _____

F Write directions from your school to your home.

_____

_____

_____

_____

UNIT 5 Our Community

CHALLENGE 3 ➤ Prepositions of Location

A Look at the map.

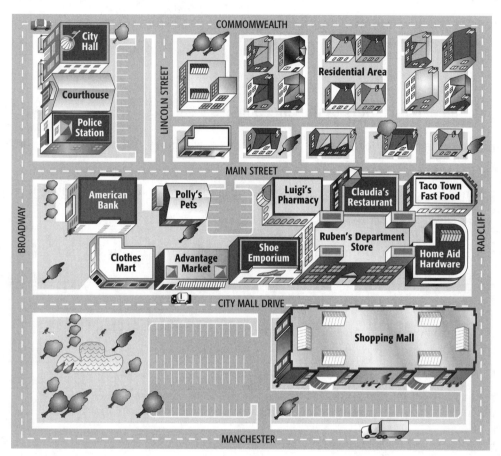

B Answer the questions. Assume that you are standing in the doorway of each location and looking out.

1. What is on the left of Shoe Emporium? _____Ruben's Department Store_____

2. What is on the right of Luigi's Pharmacy? _____

3. What is on the left of Luigi's Pharmacy? _____

4. What is on the right of Claudia's Restaurant? _____

C Practice the conversation with locations from the map in Exercise A.

Student A: Excuse me. I'm lost. Can you help me?
Student B: Sure. How can I help you?
Student A: Where's <u>Polly's Pets</u>?
Student B: It's around the corner from Clothes Mart.

D Look at the examples of prepositions.

Prepositions			
The ball is **in** the box.		The ball is **between** two boxes.	
The ball is **on** the box.		The ball is **over** the box.	
The ball is **under** the box.		The ball is **in front of** the box.	
The ball is **next to** the box.		The ball is **behind** the box.	

• Use prepositions to talk about where things are.

E Using the map in Exercise A, complete the sentences with prepositions.

1. Clothes Mart is _____next to_____ Advantage Market.

2. The shopping mall is _____ Ruben's Department Store.

3. Claudia's Restaurant is _____ Ruben's Department Store.

4. Taco Town is _____ Radcliff and Main Street.

5. Luigi's Pharmacy is _____ Polly's Pets and Claudia's Restaurant.

6. Taco Town is _____ Home Aid Hardware.

7. American Bank is _____ Polly's Pets.

8. Shoe Emporium is _____ City Mall Drive.

9. Shoe Emporium is _____ Luigi's Pharmacy.

10. Polly's Pets is _____ American Bank.

F Write sentences about your community. Use the prepositions.

1. (next to) _____

2. (across from) _____

3. (between) _____

4. (in back of) _____

5. (in front of) _____

6. (on the corner of) _____

7. (around the corner from) _____

Our Community

CHALLENGE 4 ➤ Questions with *Can*

A Look at the message.

> For *Emilio Salvador* **URGENT** ☐
> Date *June 3, 2009*   Time: *10:30* A.M. / P.M.
> **MESSAGE**
> Caller *Eric Saunders*
> of *Anderson Adult School*
> Phone *714-555-6745*
> Fax *714-555-6746*
> Message *Please call back. He needs some information. He also has an important question.*

B Answer the questions about the message.

1. Who is the call for? _____Emilio Salvador_____

2. Who is calling? _____

3. When did Eric call? _____

4. What is Eric's phone number? _____

5. What does Eric need? _____

C Read the chart.

Questions with *Can*			
Can	**Subject**	**Base**	**Example question**
can	I / you	help	**Can** you help me?
		ask	**Can** I ask you a question?
		talk	**Can** I talk to you?
		answer	**Can** you answer a question?
		call	**Can** you call me?

D Put the words in the correct order to form questions.

1. you / can / help/ I _____ Can I help you?

2. can / you / the teacher / talk / to _____

3. I / can / your questions / answer _____

4. see / you / can / I / tomorrow _____

5. a question / I / can / you / ask _____

6. call / you / can / I _____

E Rewrite the sentences into questions.

1. You can answer the phones.

   Can you answer the phones? _____

2. I can talk to you now.

   _____

3. You can help me.

   _____

4. You can ask questions.

   _____

5. I can send packages in the mail.

   _____

6. You can ask for information.

   _____

F Write the conversation in the correct order.

John: Yes. I can talk to you then.
Silvia: OK.
John: Can you call me tomorrow?
John: Hello Silvia. Can you help me?
Silvia: OK. Can I call at 3:00?
Silvia: Of course. What can I do to help?

John: ___ Hello Silvia. Can you help me? ___
Silvia: _____
John: _____
Silvia: _____
John: _____
Silvia: _____

G Write out a message you could leave on an answering machine for a friend. Use the situations below.

1. You need to talk: _____

2. You have a question: _____

3. You want to answer a question: _____

Our Community

CHALLENGE 5 ➤ Simple Present/Present Continuous

A Read the letter.

Dear Ruben,

    How are you? I am fine. I am writing you this letter because I want to tell you about my new neighborhood. I live in Angle Creek, Minnesota. I go to school almost every day. I often walk to school. I sometimes eat lunch around the corner from the school.

    I am studying English in school. I am learning to read and write in English. The students help me study. I always read the book and I always prepare for class.

    My English is good now. Can you visit me soon? I hope so.

Your friend,
Natalie

B Complete the sentences.

1. Natalie lives in <u>Angle Creek, Minnesota</u> _____.

2. She is studying _____.

3. She often _____ to school.

C Read the charts.

Simple Present			
Subject	**Adverb**	**Verb**	**Example sentence**
I	always often sometimes rarely never	write	I always **write** postcards.
you, we, they		read	They never **read** the newspaper.
he, she, it		eat	He rarely **eats** here.

100%		50%		0%
always	often	sometimes	rarely	never

Present Continuous				
Subject	***Be***	**Base +*ing***		**Example sentence**
I	am (I'm)	writing	right now	I'm **writing** a letter right now.
you, we, they	are (They're)	reading		They're **reading** a book today.
he, she, it	is (she's)	eating	today	She's **eating** a sandwich.

D Look at the pictures and complete the sentences.

Present Continuous

1. The men _____ are wearing _____ suits.

2. The boy _____ a sandwich.

3. The girls _____.

4. The woman _____.

5. The boys _____.

6. The man _____.

Simple Present

1. They _____ wear _____ suits to work.

2. He _____ a sandwich for lunch.

3. They always _____ in the mall.

4. She often _____ in a chair.

5. They _____ during recess.

6. He sometimes _____ a newspaper.

E Ask a partner the questions about the pictures in Exercise D.

Student A: What are the men wearing?
Student B: They are **wearing** suits.

Student A: What is the boy eating?
Student B:

Student A: What do the men wear to work?
Student B:

Student A: What does the man read?
Student B:

Student B: Where is the woman sitting?
Student A: She is **sitting** in a chair.

Student B: What do the boys do at recess?
Student A:

Student B: What is the man doing?
Student A:

Student B: Where do the girls walk?
Student A:

F Complete the paragraph about you and your community.

Dear _____,

How are you? I am fine. I want to tell you about my neighborhood. I live in _____. Right now I am going to school at _____. My class starts at _____. I always _____ to school. I _____ English.

UNIT 5 — Our Community

EXTENSION CHALLENGE 1 ➤ *In/On/At*

In/On/At

 A Read the information.

 B Write the information from Exercise A in the chart.

	Duong	Eva
1. Country	United States	United States
2. State		
3. City		
4. Street		
5. Birth date		

C Read the chart.

in/on/at		
Preposition		**Example sentence**
in	(country)	My family lives **in** Guatemala.
in	(state)	I live **in** California.
in	(city)	I live **in** San Diego.
on	(street)	I live **on** First Street.
at	(address)	I live **at** 5564 First Street.

D Complete the sentences with the correct prepositions.

1. I live ___at___ 3345 W. Main Street.

2. She works _____ Anaheim.

3. They have a house _____ Tampa.

4. There is a store _____ Main.

5. I live _____ Mexico and visit the U.S.

6. My store is _____ 9935 Martin Lane.

7. My sister lives _____ Portugal.

8. You are _____ New York, right?

9. Omar has a shop _____ Beach Blvd.

10. Vinicio lives _____ 4563 Park Ave.

11. My family all lives _____ Florida.

12. We go to school _____ Los Angeles.

E Write sentences about the information in Exercise B.

1. Duong lives in the United States. _____

2. Duong _____

3. Duong _____

4. Duong _____

5. Duong _____

6. Eva _____

7. Eva _____

8. Eva _____

F Write five sentences about where you live and five sentences about a partner.

1. I live in _____.

2. I _____.

3. I _____.

4. I _____.

5. I _____.

6. _____

7. _____

8. _____

9. _____

10. _____

In/On/At

UNIT 5 Our Community

EXTENSION CHALLENGE 2 ➤ Modal: *Can* (Ability)

 A **Read the paragraph.**

　　Mario is 18 years old and new in the United States. He wants to learn how to do many things. He wants to learn to speak English, drive a car, and find work. Mario knows how to send packages and take buses to different places in the city. He doesn't know how to read in English. Mario wants to learn how to ask questions in stores and talk to salespeople. He can buy things, but he can't ask questions.

 B **Complete the chart.**

Mario knows how to . . .	Mario doesn't know how to . . .
send packages	speak English

C **Read the chart.**

Modal: *Can* (Ability)			
Subject	***Can***	**Base verb**	**Example sentences**
I, you, he, she, it, we, they	can	go	I **can go** to the market.
		help	You **can help** me with the work.
		speak	He **can speak** English.
		write	She **can write** a letter in English.
		read	We **can read** the newspaper.
		talk	They **can talk** to the teacher.

D Bubble in the correct answers.

1. John _____ a car.   ● can drive   ○ can drives   ○ is drives
2. John and Kathy _____ a house.   ○ can buy   ○ are buy   ○ is buying
3. I _____ in English.   ○ can read   ○ reads   ○ reading
4. We _____ letters.   ○ can write   ○ can writes   ○ writing
5. She _____ the teacher.   ○ can helps   ○ can help   ○ helping
6. You _____ to a new house.   ○ are move   ○ can moves   ○ can move
7. They _____ to work.   ○ can drive   ○ can drives   ○ driving
8. I can _____ around the corner.   ○ eat   ○ eats   ○ eating

E Complete the sentences with *can* and the verb.

1. I __can__ __sleep__ (sleep) in the garage.
2. They _____ _____ (read) the newspaper in English.
3. Silvia and I _____ _____ (look) for a new house.
4. You _____ _____ (talk) to a real estate agent.
5. He _____ _____ (give) you directions to the bus station.
6. The students _____ _____ (follow) directions.

F Write sentences about what Mario can do. Use the information in Exercises A and B.

1. Mario can send packages. _____
2. _____
3. _____

G Check (✓) what you can do.

_____ take the bus   _____ give directions in English
_____ send packages   _____ drive a car
_____ talk to sales people in English   _____ ask questions in a store in English
_____ follow directions in English   _____ open a bank account

H Write sentences about what you can do.

1. I can _____
2. _____
3. _____
4. _____

CHALLENGE 1 ➤ Simple Present: *Hurt*

 Talk to a partner about the picture.

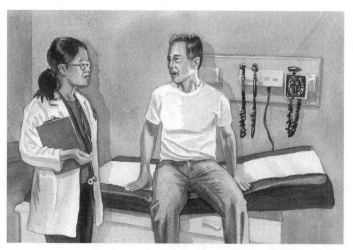

 Practice the conversation with a partner.

Doctor: Hello, Victor. What's the problem?
Victor: Doctor, I am very sick.
Doctor: You don't look well.
Victor: My legs hurt, my chest hurts, and my back hurts.
Doctor: I will give you a checkup and see what the problem is.
Victor: OK, thanks.

 Read the chart.

Simple Present: *Hurt*		
Subject	**Verb**	**Example sentence**
it my leg my arm my foot my head	hurts	My leg **hurts**. My arm **hurts**. My head **hurts**.
they my legs my arms my feet my ears	hurt	My legs **hurt**. My feet **hurt**. My ears **hurt**.

Simple Present: Hurt

Circle the correct word.

1. My back **hurt /** (**hurts**). I think I need to rest.

2. His legs **hurt / hurts**. He needs aspirin.

3. I think there is a problem with the food. My stomach **hurt / hurts**.

4. The doctor says I have the flu. That is why my head **hurt / hurts**.

5. I am reading a very long book. My eyes **hurt / hurts**.

6. I am walking to school. It is difficult because my legs **hurt / hurts**.

7. Jason's ears **hurt / hurts**. I think he needs to see the doctor.

8. I am wearing new shoes and my feet **hurt / hurts**.

 Read the information.

Gilberto

Pain: legs, hips, back

Marie

Pain: throat, ears, head

Hiep

Pain: head, eyes, sinuses, chest

 Write sentences about Gilberto, Marie, and Hiep.

EXAMPLE: _Gilberto's hip hurts._ _____

1. Marie _____

2. Her _____

3. Hiep's _____

4. His _____

5. His _____

6. Gilberto's _____

 Write a conversation with a partner. Use Exercise B as an example.

Doctor: _____

Marie: _____

Doctor: _____

Marie: _____

Doctor: _____

Marie: _____

Health and Fitness

CHALLENGE 2 ➤ Simple Present: *Have*

A Read the graph.

**Annual Health Issues
Jorge Macias**

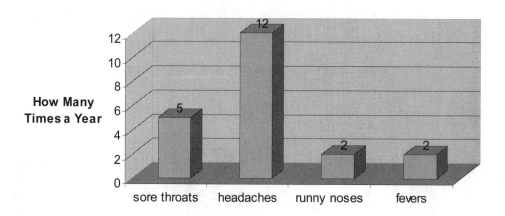

B Answer the questions about Jorge.

1. How many headaches does Jorge have every year? _____12_____

2. How many sore throats does he have? _____

3. How many fevers does he have? _____

4. How many runny noses does he have? _____

C Read the charts.

Affirmative Simple Present: *Have*		
Subject	***Have***	**Example sentence**
I, you, we, they	have	I **have** a headache. You **have** a sore throat.
he, she, it	has	She **has** a stomachache. He **has** a fever.

Negative Simple Present: *Have*			
Subject	**Negative**	***Have***	**Example sentence**
I, you, we, they	do not (don't)	have	I **don't have** a headache. You **don't have** a sore throat.
he, she, it	does not (doesn't)	have	She **doesn't have** a stomachache. He **doesn't have** a fever.

Circle the correct word.

1. Guillermo's head hurts. He **has** / **have** a headache.

2. Omar's back hurts. He **has** / **have** a backache.

3. My throat hurts. I **has** / **have** a sore throat.

4. We need a doctor. We **has** / **have** stomachaches.

5. My children are sick. They **has** / **have** earaches.

6. I don't need a doctor. I don't **has** / **have** a headache.

7. She is very healthy. She **don't** / **doesn't** have any problems.

8. I think it is a cold. You don't **have** / **has** a fever.

 Rewrite the sentences in the negative simple present.

1. They have a fever. They don't have a fever.

2. She has a sore throat. _____

3. We have colds. _____

4. I have a stomachache. _____

5. Marco has a headache. _____

6. You have the flu. _____

F **Read the information.**

Symptom	Guillermo	Antonio	Maritza
sore throat	three times a year	two times a year	four times a year
headache	one time a year	twenty times a year	ten times a year
runny nose	two times a year	six times a year	eight times a year
fever	one time a year	four times a year	three times a year

G **Write sentences using the information in Exercise F.**

1. Guillermo has a sore throat three times a year.

2. _____

3. _____

4. _____

 Complete the chart about you and a partner.

Symptom	You	Your partner
sore throat		
headache		
runny nose		
fever		

Health and Fitness

CHALLENGE 3 ➤ Modal: *Should*

A Read the medicine labels.

B Circle the best answers.

1. How many tablets do adults take?
   a. 2 to 3
   b. 1 to 2
   c. four hours

2. Children with the flu should not take it.
   a. true   b. false

3. What is this medicine for?
   a. for runny noses
   b. for aches and pains
   c. for stomachaches

4. You can take 24 tablets in one day.
   a. true   b. false

C Read the charts.

Modal: *Should*			
Subject	***Should***	**Base verb**	**Example sentence**
I, you, he, she, it, we, they	should	rest stay go take	You **should** rest. He **should** stay home. They **should** go to the doctor. I **should** take pain relievers. We **should** take cough syrup.

Modal: *Should* (Negative)			
Subject	***Should***	**Base verb**	**Example sentence**
I, you, he, she, it, we, they	should not (shouldn't)	drive drink go	You **shouldn't drive** and take this medicine. He **shouldn't drink** alcohol with this medicine. We **shouldn't go** out.

D Complete the sentences.

1. She _____should eat_____ (eat) after taking this medicine.

2. You _____ (get) a lot of sleep and rest.

3. They _____ (no/take) the medicine if they have the flu.

4. Nancy and Margie _____ (no/drink) when taking this medicine.

5. I _____ (no/go) to work. I am sick.

6. We _____ (take) two tablets three times a day.

7. Karen _____ (take) cough syrup for her sore throat.

8. He _____ (see) a doctor right now.

E Read the labels.

COUGH SYRUP

Usage: For temporary relief of cough and sore throat irritation due to infections.

Directions: Take two teaspoons every four hours for pain.

Warning: Don't take if you are pregnant.

Antacid Tablets

Usage: For fast relief of acid indigestion and stomach pain.

Directions: Take two to four tablets as needed.

Warning: Don't give this medicine to children.

F With a partner, practice the conversation with information from Exercises E and A.

Student A: Can you help me?
Student B: Sure.
Student A: What medicine should I take?
Student B: You should take this aspirin.
Student A: How much should I take?
Student B: You should take one to two tablets every four hours.
Student A: Thanks.
Student B: Oh, you shouldn't give it to children.

G Complete the chart with a group. What medicine should you take?

Headache	Stomachache	Sore throat	Aches and pains	Cough

Health and Fitness

CHALLENGE 4 ➤ *Who, What, Where*

Who, What, Where

A Read the paragraph.

There is a house on fire at 2245 Adam Street in Costa Mesa. It is an emergency. There are three people in the house and the fire fighters are helping them. The fire is very hot. The three people are Jim, Kathy, and Lucy Hamilton. It is now 3:30 P.M. and the fire is intense!

B Complete the sentences about the fire.

1. Jim, Kathy, and Lucy Hamilton live at _____ 2245 Adam Street _____.

2. The fire is in the city of _____.

3. It is _____ in the afternoon.

4. _____ people are in the house.

5. The fire fighters are helping _____,

_____, and _____.

C Read the chart.

Question word	Verb	Example question	Example answer
What	is	**What** is the emergency?	There is a fire! There is an accident. A house is on fire. My father is having a heart attack.
Where	is	**Where** is the emergency?	On First Street. Here in my house. At 1432 W. Palm Street.
Who	is calling is talking is in trouble	**Who** is calling? **Who** is talking? **Who** is in trouble?	John. John. My father, Eric Ludlow.

D Fill in the blank with the correct word. Use *Who*, *What*, or *Where*.

1. ___Where___ is the fire? It's on First Street, next to the market.

2. _____ is the problem? My son has a broken arm.

3. _____ is the emergency? We need assistance. There is a car accident.

4. _____ is in trouble? My brother is having a heart attack.

5. _____ is the accident? It is on the corner of Maple and Birch Street.

6. _____ is calling? My name is Roger Dunn.

7. _____ is the matter? My house is on fire!

E Read the emergency calls.

| 1. A house is on fire at 3234 Maple Street. My name is Claudia. Please hurry! |

| 2. I am Greg LeBonte. I live on Sycamore Street. There is a car in my living room! |

| 3. There is an accident on Main Street and McFadden. Please hurry. My name is Annabelle and my phone number is 555-6754. |

| 4. Please send the paramedics immediately to 7774 W. Harbor Blvd. My Father is having a heart attack. His name is Oscar Mejia. |

F Complete the chart with the information from Exercise E.

Who	What	Where
1. Claudia	house on fire	3234 Maple Street
2.		
3.		
4.		

G Write a new emergency call. Use Exercise E as a model.

Health and Fitness

CHALLENGE 5 ➤ *Want to*

A Read the bar graph.

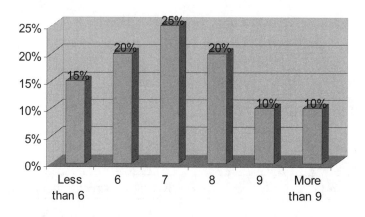

Alta, Wisconsin (Average Sleep Per Night)

B Answer the questions about the bar graph.

1. What percentage of people sleep seven hours every night? ___**25%**___

2. What percentage of people sleep more than nine hours? _____

3. What percentage of people sleep six hours every night? _____

4. How many hours do you sleep? _____

5. What number of hours is healthy? _____

C Read the chart.

Want to			
Subject	**Verb**	**Infinitive** (*to* + base)	**Example sentence**
I, you, we, they	want	to	run exercise walk
			I **want to run**. We **want to exercise**. They **want to walk**.
he, she, it	wants		ride do go eat sleep
			He **wants to ride** a bicycle. She **wants to do** yard work. She **wants to go** to the gym. Oscar **wants to eat** three meals a day. Maria **wants to sleep** eight hours a night.

D Write *want to* or *wants to*.

1. The woman _____wants to_____ exercise one hour every day.

2. We _____ make goals for our health.

3. They _____ eat three meals a day.

4. I _____ sleep seven or eight hours every day.

5. Luz _____ run in the morning for three miles two times a week.

6. Paula and I _____ ride bikes every day for three miles.

7. I _____ walk around the block every evening with my husband.

8. He _____ go to the gym on Mondays and Wednesdays.

9. Eva _____ exercise in the morning and sleep eight hours at night.

10. We _____ walk to school every day.

E Read the goal chart.

Name	Sleep	Exercise	Meals
Martha	8 hours	20 minutes	3 meals
Kimberly	7 hours	1 hour	2 meals
Luis	7 hours	45 minutes	3 meals

F Write sentences about the goals in Exercise E.

1. Martha wants to sleep eight hours every night _____.

2. Martha _____.

3. Martha _____.

4. Kimberly and Luis _____.

5. Martha and Luis _____.

G What are your goals for sleep, meals, and exercise? Write your goals and your partner's goals. Then, report to a group.

1. I want to _____

2. _____

3. _____

4. My partner wants to _____

5. _____

6. _____

EXTENSION CHALLENGE 1 ➤ *Yes/No Questions with Should*

Yes/No Questions with Should

 Match the problem with the advice. Draw a line.

1. My father is having a heart attack!

2. I have a cough.

3. I have a terrible headache.

4. My sister has a bad stomachache.

a. You should take some throat lozenges.

b. You should take a pain reliever.

c. You should give her some antacid tablets.

d. You should call 911 immediately!

 Practice different conversations with a partner. Use the information from Exercise A.

Student A: What's the matter?
Student B: My father is having a heart attack!
Student A: You should call 911 immediately.

C Read the chart.

Yes/No Questions with *Should*			
Should	Subject	Base verb	Example question and answer
should	I, you, he, she, it, we, they	take	**Should** she take medicine? Yes, she should.
		call	**Should** I call 911? Yes, you should!
		give	**Should** they give her medicine? No, they shouldn't.

D · Write questions with the words.

1. I / call / 911 / should _____ Should I call 911? _____

2. should / give / you / him / medicine _____

3. they / rest / should / get / some _____

4. should / we / aspirin / take _____

5. he / should / every day / exercise _____

6. talk / should / she / to the doctor _____

E · Answer the questions.

1. My son is very ill with a 105 degree fever. Should I call 911?

   Yes, you should. _____

2. A cat is in a tree. Should I call 911?

   _____

3. He accidentally took poison. Should we call 911?

   _____

4. She is having a heart attack! Should we call 911?

   _____

5. We are very tired. Should we call 911?

   _____

6. They are sick with the flu. Should they call 911?

   _____

F · Read the problem and write a question. Then, ask a partner.

1. I have a stomachache. Should I take antacid tablets? _____

2. I am having a heart attack. _____

3. I am very tired. _____

4. I like coffee. _____

5. I need a checkup. _____

Health and Fitness

EXTENSION CHALLENGE 2 ➤ *Wh-* Questions with *Should*

A Read the conversation.

Margaret: I have a few problems and I don't know what to do.
Antonio: Maybe I can help. What are the problems?
Margaret: My daughter is sick. What should I do?
Antonio: You should take her to see the doctor.
Margaret: Where should I go?
Antonio: My doctor is good. Take her to my doctor's office.

B Answer the questions about the conversation.

1. Is Margaret's son sick? _____ No _____

2. Is Margaret sick? _____

3. Who is Margaret talking to? _____

4. What is Margaret's problem? _____

C Read the chart.

Wh- Questions with *Should*				
Question word	*Should*	Subject	Base verb	Example sentence
what when where who what time how long how much how many	should	I, you, he, she, it, we, they	do take go call give stay	What **should** I do? When **should** I take the medicine? Where **should** they go for help? Who **should** we call? What time **should** I take the medicine? How long **should** you stay in bed? How much medicine **should** I give her? How many tablets **should** she take?

Wh- Questions with *Should*

Complete the questions with a word or phrase from the box. Use each one only once.

how much	how many	how long	~~when~~
where	who	what	what time

1. _____ When _____ should I ask for the medicine?

2. _____ should I call the ambulance?

3. _____ should they call in an emergency?

4. _____ should they go for assistance?

5. _____ water should I drink with the medicine?

6. _____ tablets should I take?

7. _____ should they exercise?

8. _____ do I do in an emergency?

 Use two questions from Exercise D. Make a conversation and practice with a partner.

Student A: _____

Student B: _____

Student A: _____

Student B: _____

Student A: _____

Student B: _____

F **You have the flu. You have questions for the doctor. Write questions with the information and *should*.**

1. what time / take / my medicine

   What time should I take my medicine? _____

2. when / call/ the health insurance company

   _____

3. what / eat / today

   _____

4. how long / stay / in bed

   _____

5. how much / cough medicine / take

   _____

Working on It

CHALLENGE 1 ➤ Simple Present

A Read the information.

Natalia is
a carpenter.

Esteban is
a delivery person.

Kristina is a computer
programmer.

Phuong is
a homemaker.

B List the inside and outside jobs.

Inside	Outside

C List jobs that require special education.

Special Education	No Special Education

D Read the charts.

Affirmative Simple Present		
Subject	**Verb**	**Example sentence**
I, you, we, they	work	I **work**. I **work** inside. We **work** in an office. They **work** in a store.
he, she, it	works	He **works** outside. She **works** inside.

Negative Simple Present			
Subject	**Negative**	**Verb**	**Example sentence**
I, you, we, they	don't	work	I **don't work** outside. We **don't work** in an office. They **don't work** in a store.
he, she, it	doesn't	work	He **doesn't work** in an office. She **doesn't work** in a store.

E Complete the sentences with the correct form of *work*.

1. Ramiro is a doctor. He _____ doesn't work _____ in a supermarket.

2. The brothers are mechanics. They _____ at Adel's Clothing.

3. I am an assembler. I _____ in a factory.

4. We are homemakers. We _____ at Centennial Adult School.

5. You are a babysitter. You _____ with children.

6. Ly sleeps from 6:00 A.M.–12:00 P.M. She _____ in the morning.

F Read the information.

Name	Store	Factory	Office	Outside	Car	Home
Chen, Alan, and Oscar		X				
Benjamin	X					
Tien			X			
Peter and Sally				X		
Tino, Maria, and Gaspar						X
Ron					X	

G Write sentences about where the people in Exercise F work.

1. Chen, Alan, and Oscar _work in a factory_____.

2. Benjamin _____.

3. Tien _____.

4. Peter and Sally _____.

5. Tino, Maria, and Gaspar _____.

6. Ron _____.

H Talk to three classmates.

Name	Where do you work?
1.	
2.	
3.	

Working on It

CHALLENGE 2 ➤ Modal: *Can* (Ability)

A Look at the classified ads.

DAILY NEWS *Classified Ads*

EMPLOYMENT

Apartment Manager
FT, 2 yrs exp, free rent, speak Spanish and English, paint and minor maintenance. Available immediately.
Call Manor Apartments, 555-8976.

Full-Time Cook
No experience needed, training available, Martha's Kitchen, good hours, apply in person, 3456 W. Melrose, Hill City, 8am-5pm

Legal Assistant
45 wpm, filing, speak English, FT, great opportunity, Smith and Peterson Law Office. Call 555-9988.

B Complete the chart with information from Exercise A.

Position	Experience?	F/T or P/T
Apartment Manager		

C Read the charts.

Modal: *Can* (Ability)			
Subject	***Can***	**Verb**	**Example sentence**
I, you, he, she, it, we, they	can	drive	I **can** drive a truck.
		speak	You **can** speak English well.
		talk	He **can** talk to customers.
		collect	We **can** collect money.
		clean	They **can** clean the offices.

Can (Negative)			
Subject	***Can***	**Verb**	**Example sentence**
I, you, he, she, it, we, they	cannot (can't)	drive	I **can't** drive a truck.
		speak	You **can't** speak English well.
		talk	He **can't** talk to customers.
		collect	We **can't** collect money.
		clean	They **can't** clean the offices.

D Each sentence contains a mistake. Rewrite the sentences correctly with *can*.

1. He cans drive a truck. <u>He can drive a truck.</u>

2. My sister can to calculate numbers quickly. _____

3. She cans type very well. _____

4. She can in a factory work. _____

5. They no can talk on the phone. _____

6. Miyuki no work outside. _____

E Look at the diagram.

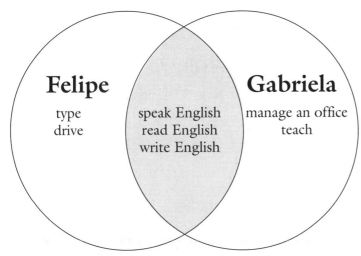

Felipe
type
drive

speak English
read English
write English

Gabriela
manage an office
teach

F Write sentences about what Felipe and Gabriela *can* and *can't* do.

1. Felipe can <u>type letters</u> _____.

2. Felipe can't _____.

3. Gabriela can _____.

4. Gabriela can't _____.

5. Felipe and Gabriela can _____.

6. Felipe and Gabriela can _____.

G Write what you *can* and *can't* do.

_____

_____

Working on It

CHALLENGE 3 ➤ Simple Past (regular) and *Was/Were*

A Read Nathan's job history section of an application.

POSITION	COMPANY	FROM	TO	DUTIES (responsibilities)
Supervisor	Archer's Furniture	05-2007	05-2008	managed ten workers
Delivery person	Archer's Furniture	01-2004	04-2007	delivered furniture
Assembler	Tricon Industries	10-2002	01-2004	assembled parts to radios

B Answer the questions about the job history in Exercise A.

1. Where did Nathan work in 2005? _Nathan worked at Archer's Furniture._

2. When did he work in Tricon Industries? _____

3. What job did he have in May 2007? _____

4. What were his responsibilities in 2003? _____

C Read the charts.

Simple Past: Regular Verbs			
Subject	**Base + *ed***		**Example sentence**
I, you, he, she, it, we, they	cleaned	tables	I **cleaned** tables.
	cooked	hamburgers	You **cooked** hamburgers.
	prepared	breakfast	He **prepared** breakfast.
	delivered	packages	She **delivered** packages.
	counted	the money	It **counted** the money.
	helped	other workers	We **helped** other workers.
	moved	to the United States	They **moved** to the United States.

Simple Past: *Be*			
Subject	**Be**		**Example sentence**
I, he, she, it	was	a mail carrier	I **was** a mail carrier.
we, you, they	were	happy	You **were** happy.

D Complete the sentences with the correct simple past tense form of the verbs.

1. I ___was___ a mechanic. I ___repaired___ (repair) cars.

2. She _____ an assembly worker. She _____ (assemble) furniture.

3. We _____ mail carriers. We _____ (deliver) mail.

4. You _____ a secretary. You _____ (type) letters.

5. They _____ servers at a restaurant. They _____ (talk) to customers.

6. Juana and I _____ managers. We _____ (supervise) workers.

7. Sherrie _____ a cook. She _____ (serve) food for La Roma Restaurant.

8. You _____ a cashier. You _____ (count) money for the store.

E Read the information.

Name	Before	Now
Mario	office worker / type letters	student / study English
Gabriela	teacher / help students	writer / write books
Rex	mechanic / repair cars	driver / drive a taxi
Pam	mail carrier / deliver letters	sales person / sell computers

F Write sentences with the information in Exercise E.

1. Mario is a student. He studies English. He was an office worker. He typed letters.

2. Gabriela _____

   _____.

3. Rex _____

   _____.

4. Pam _____

   _____.

G Complete a job history for a partner and report to a group.

Position	Company	From	To	Duties (responsibilities)

CHALLENGE 4 ➤ Questions with *Can*

A Read the information.

Job	mops	answers phones	talks to customers	types letters	takes breaks	files papers
Salesperson		x	x		x	
Administrative assistant		x		x	x	x
Receptionist		x	x		x	x
Custodian	x				x	

B Circle *True* or *False*.

1. A salesperson sometimes answers phones.
   (True)
   False

2. A receptionist mops the floor.
   True
   False

3. An administrative assistant types.
   True
   False

4. A custodian files papers.
   True
   False

5. A sales person talks to customers.
   True
   False

6. A receptionist types letters.
   True
   False

C Read the chart.

Questions with *Can*			
Can	**Subject**	**Verb**	**Example questions and answers**
can	I, you, he, she, it, we, they	type drive talk work understand cook clean	**Can** you type letters? Yes, I can. **Can** they drive a car? No they can't. **Can** she understand English? Yes, she can. **Can** I work on Saturdays? Yes, you can. **Can** he cook breakfast? No, he can't. **Can** we clean on the weekend? Yes, you can. **Can** you talk to customers? No, you can't.

D Make questions with the words and *can*.

1. type / you / letters   <u>Can you type letters?</u>

2. speak / they / English   _____

3. I / work / every week   _____

4. we / talk / to the supervisor   _____

5. clean / bathrooms / you   _____

6. repair / she / my car   _____

E Complete the conversation with the correct words.

Business Owner: It is nice to meet you, Javier.

Javier: It is nice to meet you, too.

Business Owner: We need a custodian and repair person.

Javier: Yes, I know. I _____ clean and I _____ do plumbing.

Business Owner: That's great. _____ you repair windows and doors?

Javier: Yes I _____.

Business Owner: You need to complete reports. _____ you _____ in English?

Javier: No, I am sorry. I am studying English in school, but I _____ ask my teacher for help with the forms.

Business Owner: Yes, I think we _____ work with that.

Javier: Thank you.

F Talk to students in the class. Answer the questions.

EXAMPLES:

Student A: Can you type?   *Student A:* Can you drive?
Student B: Yes, I can.   *Student B:* No, I can't.

1. Who can type?   _____

2. Who can drive?   _____

3. Who can file papers?   _____

4. Who can clean offices?   _____

5. Who can talk to customers in English?   _____

Simple Present/Past: *Be* + Adjectives

Working on It

CHALLENGE 5 ➤ Simple Present/Past: *Be* + Adjectives

A Read the evaluation form. List the rating for each skill.

Fairview Hotel

Employee Evaluation Form

Employee Name: Dalva Mendes
Position: Administrative Assistant
Date: April 4

EVALUATION

1. Comes to work on time	S	**G**	NI
2. Follows instructions	**S**	G	NI
3. Helps others	**S**	G	NI
4. Works well with the team	**S**	G	NI
5. Understands the job	S	G	**NI**
New employee. She is still learning.			
6. Has a positive attitude	**S**	G	NI
Enjoys her job and is always cheerful			

Supervisor's signature: *Patricia Macias*
Employee's signature: *Dalva Mendes*

S = Superior   G = Good   NI = Needs improvement

Skill	Rating
1. Comes to work on time.	G
2. Follows instructions.	_____
3. Understands the job.	_____
4. Helps others.	_____
5. Is a team player.	_____
6. Has a positive attitude.	_____

B Read the charts.

Simple Present: *Be*			
Subject	**Be**	**Adjective**	**Example sentence**
I	am	early	I **am** always early to work.
he, she	is	late	She **is** sometimes late to work.
we, you, they	are	punctual friendly neat and clean	We **are** punctual after our break. You **are** rarely friendly with the customers.

Simple Past: *Be*			
Subject	**Be**	**Adjective**	**Example sentence**
I, he, she	was	early late	I **was** always early to work. She **was** sometimes late to work.
we, you, they	were	punctual friendly neat and clean	We **were** punctual after our break. You **were** rarely friendly with the customers.

C Complete the sentences with the correct *be* verb and word from the box. Some words may be used more than once.

early	late	punctual	friendly	neat and clean

1. Dalva is always on time. She ___is___ very ___punctual___.

2. Work starts at 7:00 A.M. Maria arrives at 6:30. She _____ always _____.

3. Last year, Kevin never arrived on time. He _____ always _____.

4. Nina is often not careful when she talks. She _____ rarely _____.

5. Look at the office. It is a mess! Olga _____ never _____.

6. Nathan works hard. He has car trouble. He _____ sometimes _____ to work.

7. Martha was good with customers. She _____ always _____ with them.

8. Jim has a problem. He doesn't clean his area. He _____ never _____.

D Read Dalva's evaluation.

　　Dalva is a good worker. She is usually punctual. She is rarely late to work. She likes to help others and is always very friendly. She should take a break, but she rarely does.

　　Yesterday, I worked with Dalva. She arrived on time. She followed all instructions well. Her work area is very clean. She always answers the phone and talks to customers with a friendly smile. Yesterday, Dalva had lunch in the cafeteria. She returned to work 20 minutes early. She likes to work. Dalva is a good employee.

Patricia Macias

E Complete the sentences about Dalva's evaluation in Exercise D using the correct form of the *be* verb.

1. Dalva ___is___ usually punctual.

2. She _____ rarely late to work.

3. Dalva _____ at work on time yesterday.

4. After lunch yesterday, Dalva _____ back to work 20 minutes early.

5. Dalva's work area _____ always clean and neat.

6. Dalva _____ a good employee.

F Complete the sentences about you and school.

1. I ____ _____ _____ to school. (late / early / on time)

2. I ____ _____ _____ at school. (friendly / clean and neat)

UNIT 7 **Working on It**

EXTENSION CHALLENGE 1 ➤ Simple Past: *Be*

A Read about Lien.

My name is Lien. I am from Vietnam. In Vietnam, I was a nurse. I lived in a little city near the capital. When I arrived in the United States in 1988, I needed a job. I was a cashier for three years in a small Vietnamese clothing store. My boss was very nice and friendly. She helped me learn English. Now I am an administrative assistant. I answer phones and type letters. I think I am a good worker.

B Follow the instructions about Exercise A.

1. Underline Lien's three jobs.

2. Circle all the adjectives you see.

3. What are Lien's job responsibilities now? _____

C Read the charts.

Simple Past: *Be*			
Subject	**Be**	**Information**	**Example sentence**
I, he, she, it	was	her boss friendly a cashier	I **was** her boss. He **was** friendly. She **was** a cashier.
you, we, they	were	a police officer punctual good workers	You **were** a police officer. We **were** punctual. They **were** good workers.

Negative Simple Past: *Be*			
Subject	**Be**	**Information**	**Example sentence**
I, he, she, it	was not (wasn't)	her boss friendly a cashier	I **wasn't** her assistant. He **was** not friendly. She **was** not a cashier.
you, we, they	were (weren't)	a police officer punctual good workers	You **weren't** a policeman. We **were** not punctual. They **weren't** good workers.

D Fill in the blanks with *was* or *were*.

1. My mother _____was_____ a homemaker.

2. I _____ a doctor in my country.

3. My sister and I _____ students.

4. They _____ friendly at lunch break.

5. He _____ my assistant.

6. She _____ always punctual.

E Rewrite the sentences in Exercise D in the negative.

1. My mother wasn't a homemaker. _____

2. _____

3. _____

4. _____

5. _____

6. _____

F Kuzuhiro is asking a friend, Isabella, about her last job. Write Kuzuhiro's and Isabella's statements with the words provided and *was* or *were*.

Kuzuhiro: Were you happy at your job?

Isabella: yes / happy / I _Yes, I was happy._____

Kuzuhiro: Was it a full-time job?

Isabella: it / yes _____

Kuzuhiro: Were your coworkers friendly?

Isabella: yes / friendly / my manager / too _____

Kuzuhiro: Was the office far away?

Isabella: no / far away / it _____

Kuzuhiro: Were you a secretary?

Isabella: no / I / a receptionist _____

G Interview the teacher or a friend about his or her job in the past.

1. What was the job? _____

2. Was he or she happy in the job? _____

3. Was it a full-time job? _____

4. Were the coworkers friendly? _____

UNIT 7 Working on It

EXTENSION CHALLENGE 2 ➤ Future: *Will*

A **Read the story.**

Jane is a cook at a restaurant in Arlington, North Dakota. She likes to cook. She cooks hamburgers and prepares french fries. She will go to school next year and learn how to be a chef. She wants to make special meals and work in an expensive restaurant. Right now, she works in the afternoon. In the future, she will work at night. Jane has many goals. Today she studies English and wants a high school diploma, but next year she will have a high school diploma and a new job. Jane will study and prepare for class every day.

B **Complete the chart about Jane now and in the future.**

Now	Future
She is a cook.	

C **Read the chart.**

Future: *Will*			
Subject	***Will***	**Verb**	**Example sentence**
I, you, he, she, it, we, they	will	drive	I **will** drive a truck.
		speak	You **will** speak English well.
		talk	He **will** talk to customers.
		collect	We **will** collect money.
		type	They **will** type fast.
		be	I **will** be a nurse.

D Rewrite the sentences using the future tense.

1. I need an assistant now.

   <u>I will need an assistant in the future.</u>

2. He drives a truck and make deliveries.

   _____

3. Marjorie and Bill work on Saturdays.

   _____

4. Nate and I speak English well.

   _____

5. You type very fast.

   _____

6. He is a doctor.

   _____

E Complete the paragraph with the future tense of the verbs.

Luis is a very good worker. He _____<u>will be</u>_____ (be) a good manager. Luis _____ (have) many responsibilities. For example, he _____ (meet) with all the workers in the factory two times a week. He _____ (watch) the assembly workers carefully. He _____ (give) performance reviews. Luis understands the job and he speaks English well. He _____ (help) the workers understand their jobs well also. This is a good job for Luis. He _____ (do) a great job.

F Write true sentences about you and your work in the future. Read them to a partner.

1. _____
2. _____
3. _____
4. _____
5. _____

UNIT 8 People and Learning

CHALLENGE 1 ➤ Simple Past (Irregular Verbs)

 Read the story.

Armando worked hard and was a good student. He was always early to class. He learned a lot, and he was ready for the next level. Armando spoke English every day. He watched TV, talked to people in English and practiced all the time. He listened to the teacher's instructions carefully, and he always helped the other students.

B **Underline the past tense verbs in the story.**

 Read the chart.

Base form	Past form	Base form	Past form	Base form	Past form
become	became	give	gave	see	saw
begin	began	go	went	sell	sold
break	broke	grow	grew	send	sent
bring	brought	hang	hung	sing	sang
build	built	have	had	sit	sat
buy	bought	hear	heard	sleep	slept
catch	caught	hurt	hurt	speak	spoke
choose	chose	know	knew	spend	spent
come	came	leave	left	stand	stood
cost	cost	lose	lost	sweep	swept
cut	cut	make	made	take	took
do	did	meet	met	teach	taught
draw	drew	pay	paid	tell	told
drink	drank	put	put	think	thought
drive	drove	quit	quit	throw	threw
eat	ate	read	read*	understand	understood
feel	felt	ride	rode	wake	woke
find	found	ring	rang	wear	wore
forget	forgot	run	ran	write	wrote
get	got	say	said		

- Many verbs are irregular in the simple past tense. You need to memorize these verbs.
* The past form **read** rhymes with **red**.

D Complete each sentence with the past tense of the verb in parentheses.

1. We ____built____ (build) this road last year.

2. I _____ (hear) about the benefits.

3. We _____ (buy) suits for the interview.

4. She _____ (give) me my paycheck.

5. I _____ (hurt) my knee at work.

6. Victor _____ (wear) a hard hat.

7. She _____ (become) a doctor.

8. The custodians _____ (throw) out the trash.

9. My boss _____ (catch) a cold.

10. Beth _____ (read) her evaluation.

11. He _____ (find) a great job.

12. She _____ (know) every coworker.

13. I _____ (put) the package over there.

14. We _____ (find) the office keys.

15. He _____ (pay) the delivery person.

E Complete the paragraph with present tense and past tense verbs.

Christy is a great student. She works hard. She _____got_____ (get) to school on time every day this year. Yesterday she _____ (read) from the book. Her English is very good. She also _____ (teach) other students. She also _____ (write) a letter to the teacher yesterday. It _____ (be) in perfect English. Christy _____ (participate) in every activity, _____ (study) at home, and _____ (learn) new words all this year.

F Using five of the new verbs in the past, write true sentences about you. Then, read them to a partner.

1. _____

2. _____

3. _____

4. _____

5. _____

UNIT 8

People and Learning

CHALLENGE 2 ➤ Review: *Can*

A Read about Amanda.

Amanda is a student at Hampton Adult School. She is good at reading and writing. She studies at home and practices writing every day. She learns her grammar and vocabulary.

Amanda doesn't go to school every day. She doesn't like to practice speaking very much. She doesn't understand English when people speak. She needs some help. She doesn't like to work in a group. She needs help with life skills, too. She doesn't go out in the community. She wants to stay home and study.

B Complete the chart about Amanda.

Things Amanda does well	Things Amanda needs help with
She is good at reading.	She needs help with listening.

C Check (✓) things that Amanda can do to help her understand English.

- ☑ listen to the radio in English
- ☐ watch TV in English
- ☐ come to class every day
- ☐ help other students
- ☐ write paragraphs in English for practice
- ☐ read books in English
- ☐ study in her book
- ☐ practice in her grammar book
- ☐ talk to people at the supermarket
- ☐ study a picture dictionary
- ☐ learn new words every day
- ☐ talk to people at work in English

D Read the chart.

Modal: *Can*			
Subject	***Can***	**Base verb**	**Example sentence**
I, you, he, she, it, we, they	can	read	I **can** read the newspaper.
		study	You **can** study a picture dictionary.
		watch	He **can** watch TV in English.
		help	She **can** help other students.
		practice	We **can** practice with other students.
		talk	They **can** talk to salespeople.

E Write sentences about what Amanda *can* do to practice listening. See Exercise C.

1. She can watch TV in English.

2. _____

3. _____

F Write sentences about what Amanda *can* do to practice speaking. See Exercise C.

1. She can come to class every day.

2. _____

3. _____

4. _____

G Write sentences about what Amanda *can* do to practice teamwork. See Exercise C.

1. Help other students in her class to describe their jobs in English.

2. _____

H Write sentences about what Amanda *can* do to practice life skills. See Exercise C.

1. She can ask her grocer about her menus and shopping list.

2. _____

3. _____

I Complete the chart for your partner. Ask: *What do you need help with?*

Things my partner does well	Things my partner needs help with
He/She is good at . . .	He/She needs help with . . .

J Use the chart in Exercise I to write sentences about what your partner *can* do.

1. _____

2. _____

3. _____

UNIT 8 People and Learning

CHALLENGE 3 ➤ Review: *Should*

A Circle the schooling each person needs.

1. Marie wants to be an administrative assistant.

   ~~High School Diploma~~
   Community College
   University
   Trade School
   Go to work

2. Gilberto wants to be a chef.

   High School Diploma
   Community College
   University
   Trade School
   Go to work

3. Lien wants to be an English teacher.

   High School Diploma
   Community College
   University
   Trade School
   Go to work

4. Mario wants to be a dentist.

   High School Diploma
   Community College
   University
   Trade School
   Go to work

2. Kenji wants to be a computer technician

   High School Diploma
   Community College
   University
   Trade School
   Go to work

3. Anya wants to be a nurse.

   High School Diploma
   Community College
   University
   Trade School
   Go to work

B Read the chart.

Modal: *Should*			
Subject	**Should**	**Base verb**	**Example sentence**
I, you, he, she, it, we, they	should	go	I **should** go to college.
		attend	You **should** attend a trade school.
		study	He **should** study medicine.
		learn	We **should** learn English at an adult school.
		get	They **should** get a high school diploma.

C Complete each sentence using *should* and the correct form of the verb.

1. John and Sherry _____should go_____ (go) to a trade school.

2. Kim and I _____ (learn) English before we get high school diplomas.

3. I _____ (get) a Bachelor's degree first.

4. You _____ (attend) a trade school and then, you will get a certificate.

5. Caroline _____ (study) English and then, go to college.

6. Jennie _____ (ask) a counselor for help.

D Read the information and write a sentence to give advice.

1. I am a student at Carver Adult School. I want to learn English and get a diploma. What should I do next? I want to be a mechanic. I like to work on cars.

   You should go to a trade school._____

2. Ivan and Gregorio are students at Emory School. They want to be doctors. It will be difficult. They need more practice in English and they need more experience in school before they go to a university. Where should they go first?

   _____

3. Roxana is completing her work at Nettle's School. She wants to be a nurse. She learned that it is not necessary to have a BA to be a nurse in her state, but she needs a certificate and an AA degree. What should she do?

   _____

4. We are students at a school in Anchorage. We all want to be school teachers. We already have high school diplomas from our countries. We need BA degrees to be teachers. Where do we go?

   _____

E Ask two classmates for their goals. Then, write sentences about what they should do.

Classmate's 1 goals	Classmate's 2 goals

1. _____

   _____

2. _____

   _____

People and Learning

CHALLENGE 4 ➤ Review: *Like, Want, Need*

A Look at the job titles.

doctor	cashier	carpenter	salesperson

B Read what people like to do. Write the job title you think is best for each person.

1. Title: _____carpenter_____

   Isaac: likes to work outside, likes to work with his hands

2. Title: _____

   Maria: has a college degree, likes to help people, wants to work in a hospital

3. Title: _____

   Eva: needs a part-time job, likes to count and sort money, is very honest

4. Title: _____

   Michael: likes to talk to people, likes to work in stores, is friendly

C Read the charts.

Verb + Infinitive			
Subject	**Verb**	**Infinitive**	**Example sentence**
I you we they	like want need	to study to travel to work to talk	I **like to study.** You **want to travel.** We **need to work** alone. They **like to talk** on the phone.
he she it	likes wants needs	to work to handle to help	He **likes to handle** money. She **wants to work** outside.

Verb + Noun			
Subject	**Verb**	**Noun**	**Example sentence**
I you we they	like want need	cars computer school books food	I **like cars.** You **want a computer.** We **need books.** They **like school.**
he she it	likes wants needs		He **likes food.** She **wants a car.**

D **Complete each sentence with the correct form of the verb.**

1. Juan _____likes to work_____ (like / work) outside.

2. Martin and Janet _____ (like) computers and books.

3. Tuba _____ (want) a new car.

4. Jennifer and I _____ (need / talk) on the phone.

5. I _____ (want) a new job.

6. They _____ (like / handle) money.

7. The nurse _____ (want / help) all her patients.

8. You _____ (need) a job inside.

E **Read the information.**

Ahmed

Likes: to work at night
Needs: 8 hours of sleep, to study English
Wants: a good job

F **Complete the chart.**

Things Ahmed needs	Things Ahmed likes and wants to do
8 hours of sleep	

G **Complete the chart about you and a partner. Then, report to a group.**

Things you like, need, and want	Things you like, need, and want to do

Things my partner likes, needs, and wants	Things my partner likes, needs, and wants to do

People and Learning

CHALLENGE 5 ➤ Future: *Going to*

A Read the goals.

buy a house	have children	move to a new house
get a good job	learn English	get a better job
get married	go to college	get a diploma

B Complete the chart with the goals from Exercise A.

Family Goals	Educational Goals	Work Goals
buy a house		

C Read the charts.

Future: *Going to*			
Subject	***Going to***	**Base verb**	**Example sentence**
I	am going to (I'm going to)	learn listen	I **am going to** learn English.
you, we, they	are going to (you're / we're / they're going to)	practice read speak	We **are going to** practice English.
he, she, it	is going to (he's / she's going to)	study write	She **is going to** study English.

Future: *Going to* (Negative)			
Subject	***Going to***	**Base verb**	**Example sentence**
I	am not going to	learn listen	I **am not going to** learn English.
you, we, they	are not going to	practice read	They **are not going to** read English.
he, she, it	is not going to	speak	She **is not going to** speak English.

D **Make future plans. Complete the sentences using _be + going to._**

1. We _____are not going_____ (not / go) to a trade school.

2. Mario _____ (not / finish) high school this year.

3. He _____ (get) a Bachelor's degree.

4. I _____ (need) many new skills.

5. You _____ (like) working at night.

6. She _____ (talk) to the teacher about her goals.

7. They _____ (speak) their own language in the class.

8. We _____ (change) our jobs.

E **Look at the diagram of Angela and Vincent's goals.**

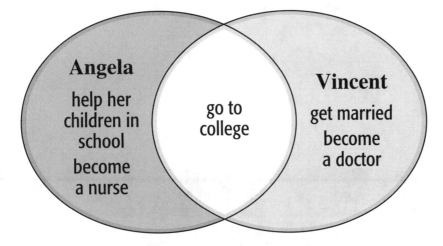

F **Write Angela and Vincent's goals using _going to._**

1. Angela is going to help her children in school. _____

2. Angela _____

3. Angela and Vincent _____

4. Vincent _____

5. Vincent _____

 G **Talk to a partner. Write his or her goals.**

1. _____

2. _____

3. _____

UNIT 8

People and Learning

EXTENSION CHALLENGE 1 ➤ Future: *Will*

(A) **Read the paragraph.**

Jessica is a student at Lake Adult School. She wants to do many things in the future, and she has many goals. She will go to school for three more years from 2008 to 2011. Then, she will go to college and get a Bachelor's degree. She will study from 2011 to 2015. She wants to be an accountant. She will take all the required classes. Jessica is a good student. She will probably study for a total of seven years.

(B) **Make a list of Jessica's goals.**

1. go to school for three more years _____
2. _____
3. _____
4. _____

(C) **Read the charts.**

Future: *Will* (Affirmative)			
Subject	**Will**	**Base verb**	**Example sentence**
I, you, we, they, he, she, it	will	read study watch help practice talk	I **will** read the newspaper. You **will** study a picture dictionary. He **will** watch TV in English. She **will** help other students. We **will** practice with other students. They **will** talk to salespeople.

Future: *Will* (Negative)				
Subject	**Will**	**Negative**	**Base verb**	**Example sentence**
I, you, we, they, he, she, it	will	not	read study watch help practice talk	I **will not** read the newspaper. You **will not** study a picture dictionary. He **will not** watch TV in English. She **will not** help other students. We **will not** practice with other students. They **will not** talk to salespeople.

D Complete the sentences with a future verb. Use the verbs in the box.

help	listen	~~read~~	talk
learn	participate	study	write

1. She _____ will read _____ the newspaper in English every day.

2. They _____ in groups.

3. He _____ to coworkers in English for practice.

4. I _____ English at home.

5. The students _____ carefully to the teacher.

6. Maria _____ in a journal every day.

7. You _____ other students.

8. I _____ four new words every day.

E Look at the paragraph in Exercise A. Complete the sentences with *will* or *won't*.

1. Jessica _____ won't _____ go to a trade school in 2011.

2. She _____ be a nurse.

3. She _____ be an accountant.

4. She _____ do many things.

5. She _____ get a Bachelor's degree.

6. She _____ study at Lake Adult School.

F What are your study goals? Use *will*.

_____

_____

_____

_____

_____

_____

_____

_____

_____

 Future: *Will*

People and Learning

EXTENSION CHALLENGE 2 ➤ Future: *Will* and *Contractions*

A Read Jan's schedule for next Monday.

Monday	
Morning	eat breakfast
	go to school
	study in the library
Afternoon	eat lunch
	visit Mom
	read my book
Evening	eat dinner
	watch TV
	go to bed

B Write four sentences about Jan's plans using *will*.

_____

_____

_____

_____

C Read the chart.

Affirmative	Contraction	Negative	Contraction	Base form
I will	I'll	I will not	I won't	**go** to college next semester.
He **will**	He'll	He **will** not	He **won't**	**ask** the teacher later.
She **will**	She'll	She will not	She **won't**	**need** a degree.
It **will**	It'll	It **will** not	It **won't**	**be** in English.
You **will**	You'll	You **will** not	You **won't**	**finish** the test.
We **will**	We'll	We **will** not	We **won't**	**look** up words at home.
They **will**	They'll	They **will** not	They **won't**	**graduate** next week.

- Use *will* + base form of a verb to talk about the future.

D Rewrite the future verbs as contractions.

EXAMPLE: You will not have time to go out.   You won't have time to go out.

1. She will not travel next year.   _____

2. I will give you a ride to school.   _____

3. It will not be easy to get experience.   _____

4. They will practice their math skills.   _____

5. He will not ask for advice.   _____

E Use the words to make future statements with *will*. Use contractions when possible.

EXAMPLE: I / move / to the city / in July   I'll move to the city in July.

1. Emir / change (negative) / his study habits

_____

2. Juan / start / college / in the fall

_____

3. I / participate / more / in class

_____

4. they / return (negative) / to Poland / next year

_____

5. my family / come / to my graduation in June

_____

F Rewrite the sentences you wrote in Exercise B with contractions.

_____

_____

_____

_____

G Write sentences about what you and a partner *will* do tomorrow.

You: _____

_____

_____

Your Partner: _____

_____

_____

➤ GLOSSARY OF GRAMMAR TERMS

adjective	a word that describes a noun (Example: the <u>red</u> hat)
adverb	a word that modifies a verb, adjective, or another adverb (Example: She eats <u>quickly</u>.)
affirmative	not negative and not a question (Example: *I like him.*)
animate/inanimate	objects that act or move (Example: <u>teacher</u> or <u>water</u>) / objects that don't act or move (Example: <u>book</u> or <u>desk</u>)
apostrophe	a punctuation mark that shows missing letters in contractions or possession (Example: *It<u>'</u>s* or *Jim<u>'</u>s*)
article	words used before a noun (Example: <u>a</u>, <u>an</u>, <u>the</u>)
base form	the main form of the verb, used without *to* (Example: <u>be</u>, <u>have</u>, <u>study</u>)
comma	the punctuation mark (,) used to indicate a pause or separation (Example: I live in an apartment**,** and you live in a house.)
complement	a word or words that add to or complete an idea after the verb (Example: He *is* <u>happy</u>.)
conjugation	the forms of a verb (Example: *I <u>am</u>, You <u>are</u>, We <u>are</u>, They <u>are</u>, He <u>is</u>, She <u>is</u>, It <u>is</u>*)
conjunction	a type of word that joins other words or phrases (Example: Maria <u>and</u> Gilberto)
consonant	any letter of the alphabet that is not a vowel (Example: B, C, D, F . . .)
continuous form	a verb form that expresses action during time (Example: *He <u>is shopping</u>.*)
contraction	shortening of a word, syllable, or word group by omission of a sound or letter (Example: It is = <u>It's</u>, does not = <u>doesn't</u>)
count nouns	nouns that can be counted by number (Example: one <u>apple</u>, two <u>apples</u>)
definite article	use of *the* when a noun is known to speaker and listener (Example: I know <u>the</u> store.)
exclamation mark	a punctuation symbol marking surprise or emotion (Example: Hello<u>!</u>)
formal	polite or respectful language (Example: <u>Could</u> you <u>please</u> give me that?)
future	a verb form in the future tense (Example: *I <u>will</u> study at that school next year.*)
imperative	a command form of a verb (Example: <u>Listen</u>! or <u>Look out</u>!)
indefinite article	*a* or *an* used before a noun when something is talked about for the first time or when *the* is too specific (Example: There's <u>a</u> new *restaurant* in town.)
infinitive	the main form of a verb, usually used with *to* (Example: I like <u>to run</u> fast.)
informal	friendly or casual language (Example: <u>Can</u> I have that?)
irregular verb	a verb different from regular form verbs (Example: be = <u>am</u>, <u>are</u>, <u>is</u>, <u>was</u>, <u>were</u>, <u>being</u>)
modal auxiliary	a verb that indicates a mood (ability, possibility, etc.) and is followed by the base form of another verb (Example: I <u>can</u> read English well.)

modifier	a word or phrase that describes another (Example: a _good friend_)
negative	the opposite of affirmative (Example: She _does not like_ meat.)
noun	a name of a person, place, or thing (Example: _Joe, England, bottle_)
non-count nouns	nouns impossible or difficult to count (Example: _water, love, rice, fire_)
object, direct	the noun or pronoun acted on by the verb (Example: I _eat oranges._)
object pronoun	replaces the noun taking the action (Example: _Julia_ is nice. I _like her._)
past tense	a verb form used to express an action or a state in the past (Example: You _worked_ yesterday.)
period	a punctuation mark of a dot ending a sentence (.)
plural	indicating more than one (Example: _pencils, children_)
possessive adjective	an adjective expressing possession (Example: _our_ car)
preposition	a word that indicates relationship between objects (Example: _on_ the _desk_)
present tense	a verb tense representing the current time, not past or future (Example: They _are_ at home right now.)
pronoun	a word used in place of a noun (Example: _Ted_ is 65. _He_ is retired.)
question form	to ask or look for an answer (Example: _Where is my book?_)
regular verb	verb with endings that are regular and follow the rule (Example: work = _work, works, worked, working_)
sentence	a thought expressed in words, with a subject and verb (Example: _Julia works hard._)
short answer	a response to a _yes/no_ question, usually a subject pronoun and auxiliary verb (Example: _Yes, I am. No he doesn't._)
singular	one object (Example: _a cat_)
statement	a sentence (Example: _The weather is rainy today._)
subject	the noun that does the action in a sentence (Example: _The gardener_ works here.)
subject pronoun	a pronoun that takes the place of a subject (Example: _John_ is a student. _He_ is smart.)
syllable	a part of a word as determined by vowel sounds and rhythm (Example: _ta-ble_)
tag questions	short informal questions that come at the end of a sentences in speech (Example: You like soup, _don't you?_ They aren't hungry, _are they?_)
tense	the part of a verb that shows the past, present, or future time (Example: He _talked._)
verb	word describing an action or state (Example: The boys _walk_ to school; I _am_ tired.)
vowels	the letters _a, e, i, o, u_, and sometimes _y_
_wh-_ questions	questions that ask for information, usually starting with _Who, What, When, Where,_ or _Why._ (Example: _Where_ do you live?) _How_ is often included in this group.
yes/no questions	questions that ask for an affirmative or a negative answer (Example: _Are you happy?_)

➤ GRAMMAR REFERENCE

Simple Present: *Be*			
Subject	**Be**	**Information**	**Example sentence**
I	am	43 years old single from Argentina from Russia married	I **am** 43 years old. (I**'m** 43 years old.)
he she	is		He **is** single. (Roberto **is** single.) She **is** from Argentina.
we you they	are		We **are** single. You **are** married. They **are** from Russia.

Negative Simple Present: *Be*			
Subject	**Verb**	**Negative**	**Example sentence (Contractions)**
I	am	not	I **am not** in the garage. (I**'m not**)
you, we, they	are		You **are not** outside. (You**'re not**) (You **aren't**) We **are not** outside. (We**'re not**) (We **aren't**) They **are not** in the kitchen. (They**'re not**) (They **aren't**)
he, she, it	is		He **is not** in the apartment. (He**'s not**) (He **isn't**) She **is not** in the apartment. (She**'s not**) (She **isn't**) It **is not** in the living room. (It**'s not**) (It **isn't**)
	Verb	**Negative**	**Example sentence (Contractions)**
There	is	not	There **is not** a front yard. (There **isn't**)
There	are		There **are not** any flowers in the backyard. (There **aren't**)

Simple Present			
Subject	**Adverb**	**Verb**	**Example sentence**
I	always often sometimes rarely never	write	I always write postcards.
you, we, they		read	They never read the newspaper.
he, she, it		eat	He rarely eats here.
100%	50%		0%
always	often	sometimes	rarely	never

Affirmative Simple Present

Subject	Verb	Example sentence
I, you, we, they	work	I **work**. I work inside. We **work** in an office. They **work** in a store.
he, she, it	works	He **works** outside. She **works** inside.

Negative Simple Present

Subject	Negative	Verb	Example sentence
I, you, we, they	don't	work	I **don't work** outside. We **don't work** in an office. They **don't work** in a store.
he, she, it	doesn't	work	He **doesn't work** in an office. She **doesn't work** in a store.

Affirmative Simple Present: *Have*

Subject	*Have*	Example sentence
I, you, we, they	have	I **have** a headache. You **have** a sore throat.
he, she, it	has	She **has** a stomachache. He **has** a fever.

Negative Simple Present: *Have*

Subject	Negative	*Have*	Example sentence
I, you, we, they	do not (don't)	have	I don't **have** a headache. You don't **have** a sore throat.
he, she, it	does not (doesn't)	have	She doesn't **have** a stomachache. He doesn't **have** a fever.

Simple Present: *Like*

Subject	Verb	Example sentence
I, you, we, they	like	I **like** hamburgers. You **like** french fries. We **like** fried chicken. They **like** roast beef.
he, she, it	likes	He **likes** cereal. She **likes** toast.

Negative Simple Present: *Like*

Subject	Negative	Verb	Noun	Example sentence
I, you, we, they	don't	like	hamburgers french fries fried chicken cereal	I **don't like** hamburgers. You **don't like** french fries.
he, she	doesn't			He **doesn't like** fried chicken. She **doesn't like** cereal.

Simple Present: *Shop*

Subject	Verb	Example sentence
I, you, we, they	shop	I **shop** for shoes at a department store. You **shop** for bread at a convenience store. We **shop** for shorts at a department store. They **shop** for books at a bookstore.
he, she, it	shops	He **shops** for shoes at a shoe store. She **shops** for dresses at a clothing store.

Simple Present: *Hurt*

Subject	Verb	Example sentence
it my leg my arm my foot my head	hurts	My leg **hurts**. My arm **hurts**. My head **hurts**.
they my legs my arms my feet my ears	hurt	My legs **hurt**. My feet **hurt**. My ears **hurt**.

Simple Present: *Want/Need*

Subject	Verb	Noun	Example sentence
I, you, we, they	want	a TV	I **want** a big TV.
	need	a book	You **need** a new book.
he, she	wants	a car	He **wants** a used car.
	needs	a shirt	She **needs** a medium shirt.

Negative Simple Present: *Want/Need*

Subject	Negative	Verb	Noun	Example sentences
I, you, we, they	don't	want need	a TV	I **don't want** a big TV.
			a book	You **don't need** a new book.
he, she	doesn't		a car	He **doesn't want** a used car.
			a shirt	She **doesn't need** a medium shirt.

Simple Present: *Live* and Prepositions

Subject	Verb	Preposition	Example sentence
I, you, we, they	live	in at on	I live **in** a house. You live **at** 4220 Greenburg St. We live **in** Miami. They live **on** First St.
he, she, it	lives	with	He lives **with** his wife. She lives **in** an apartment.

Need to

Subject	*Need*	Infinitive	Example sentence
I, you, we, they	need	to go	I **need to go** to the hospital.
		to drive	You **need to drive** to the store.
		to send	We **need to send** a letter.
		to see	They **need to see** the doctor.
he, she, it	needs	to buy	He **needs to buy** a book.
		to look for	She **needs to look for** a house.

Want to

Subject	Verb	Infinitive (*to* + base)	Example sentence
I, you, we, they	want	run exercise walk	I **want to run**. We **want to exercise**. They **want to walk**.
he, she, it	wants	to ride do go eat sleep	He **wants to ride** a bicycle. She **wants to do** yard work. She **wants to go** to the gym. Oscar **wants to eat** three meals a day. Maria **wants to sleep** eight hours a night.

Verb + Infinitive

Subject	Verb	Infinitive	Example sentence
I you we they	like want need	to study to travel to work to talk	I **like to study**. You **want to travel**. We **need to work** alone. They **like to talk** on the phone.
he she it	likes wants needs	to work to handle to help	He **likes to handle** money. She **wants to work** outside.

Verb + Noun

Subject	Verb	Noun	Example sentence
I you we they	like want need	cars computer school books food	I **like cars**. You **want a computer**. We **need books**. They **like school**.
he she it	likes wants needs		He **likes food**. She **wants a car**.

Simple Past: *Be*

Subject	*Be*	Information	Example sentence
I, he, she, it	was	her boss friendly a cashier	I **was** her boss. He **was** friendly. She **was** a cashier.
you, we, they	were	a police officer punctual good workers	You **were** a police officer. We **were** punctual. They **were** good workers.

Negative Simple Past: *Be*

Subject	*Be*	Information	Example sentence
I, he, she, it	was not (wasn't)	her boss friendly a cashier	I **wasn't** her boss. He **was** not friendly. She **was** not a cashier.
you, we, they	were (weren't)	a police officer punctual good workers	You **weren't** a police officer. We **were** not punctual. They **weren't** good workers.

Simple Past: Regular Verbs

Subject	Base + *ed*		Example sentence
I, you, he, she, it, we, they	cleaned cooked prepared delivered counted helped moved	tables hamburgers breakfast packages the money other workers to the United States	I **cleaned** tables. You **cooked** hamburgers. He **prepared** breakfast. She **delivered** packages. It **counted** the money. We **helped** other workers. They **moved** to the United States.

Present Continuous

Subject	Be	Base verb + ing	Example sentence
I	am	talk + *ing*	I **am talking** on the phone.
you, we, they	are	read + *ing* call + *ing*	We **are calling** for an appointment.
he, she, it	is	look + *ing* at look + *ing* for move + *ing*	She **is moving** into a new apartment.

Negative Present Continuous

Subject	Be		Base verb + ing	Example sentences
I	am		talk + *ing*	I **am not talking** on the phone.
you, we, they	are	not	read + *ing* call + *ing*	We **are not calling** for an appointment.
he, she, it	is		look + *ing* at look + *ing* for move + *ing*	She **is not moving** into a new apartment.

Imperatives

Subject	Verb	Information	Example sentence
~~you~~	stand up		Stand up.
~~you~~	sit down		Sit down.
~~you~~	take out	a piece of paper	Take out a piece of paper.
~~you~~	open	the book	Open the book.
~~you~~	listen to	the teacher	Listen to the teacher.
~~you~~	write	your name	Write your name.
~~you~~	help	a student	Help a student.
~~you~~	read	a book	Read a book.

	Future: *Will* (Affirmative)		
Subject	***Will***	**Base verb**	**Example sentence**
I, you, we, they, he, she, it	will	read study watch help practice talk	I **will** read the newspaper. You **will** study a picture dictionary. He **will** watch TV in English. She **will** help other students. We **will** practice with other students. They **will** talk to salespeople.

	Future: *Will* (Negative)			
Subject	***Will***	**Negative**	**Base verb**	**Example sentence**
I, you, we, they, he, she, it	will	not	read study watch help practice talk	I **will not** read the newspaper. You **will not** study a picture dictionary. He **will not** watch TV in English. She **will not** help other students. We **will not** practice with other students. They **will not** talk to salespeople.

Affirmative	**Contraction**	**Negative**	**Contraction**	**Base form**
I **will**	I'll	I **will** not	I **won't**	**go** to college next semester.
He **will**	He'll	He **will** not	He **won't**	**ask** the teacher later.
She **will**	She'll	She **will** not	She **won't**	**need** a degree.
It **will**	It'll	It **will** not	It **won't**	**be** in English.
You **will**	You'll	You **will** not	You **won't**	**finish** the test.
We **will**	We'll	We **will** not	We **won't**	**look** up words at home.
They **will**	They'll	They **will** not	They **won't**	**graduate** next week.

- Use *will* + base form of a verb to talk about the future.

Modal: *Should*

Subject	*Should*	Base verb	Example sentence
I, you, he, she, it, we, they	should	rest stay go take	You **should** rest. He **should** stay home. They **should** go to the doctor. I **should** take pain relievers. We **should** take cough syrup.

Modal: *Should* (Negative)

Subject	*Should*	Base verb	Example sentence
I, you, he, she, it, we, they	should not (shouldn't)	drive drink go	You **shouldn't** drive and take this medicine. He **shouldn't** drink alcohol with this medicine. We **shouldn't** go out.

Wh- Questions with *Should*

Question word	*Should*	Subject	Base verb	Example sentence
what when where who what time how long how much how many	should	I, you, he, she, it, we, they	do take go call give stay	What **should** I do? When **should** I take the medicine? Where **should** they go for help? Who **should** we call? What time **should** I take the medicine? How long **should** you stay in bed? How much medicine **should** I give her? How many tablets **should** she take?

Yes/No Questions with *Should*

Should	Subject	Base verb	Example question and answer
should	I, you, he, she, it, we, they	take call give	**Should** she take medicine? Yes, she should. **Should** I call 911? Yes, you should! **Should** they give her medicine? No, they shouldn't.

Modal: *Can* (Ability)

Subject	*Can*	Verb	Example sentence
I, you, he, she, it, we, they	can	drive speak talk collect clean	I **can** drive a truck. You **can** speak English well. He **can** talk to customers. We **can** collect money. They **can** clean the offices.

Can (Negative)

Subject	*Can*	Verb	Example sentence
I, you, he, she, it, we, they	cannot (can't)	drive speak talk collect clean	I **can't** drive a truck. You **can't** speak English well. He **can't** talk to customers. We **can't** collect money. They **can't** clean the offices.

Questions with *Can*

Can	Subject	Verb	Example questions and answers
can	I, you, he, she, it, we, they	type drive talk work understand cook clean	**Can** you type letters? Yes, I can. **Can** they drive a car? No they can't. **Can** she understand English? Yes, she can. **Can** I work on Saturdays? Yes, you can. **Can** he cook breakfast? No, he can't. **Can** we clean on the weekend? Yes, you can. **Can** you talk to customers? No, you can't.

Future: *Going to*

Subject	*Going to*	Base verb	Example sentence
I	am going to (I'm going to)	learn listen	I **am going to** learn English.
you, we, they	are going to (you're / we're / they're going to)	practice read speak	We **are going to** practice English.
he, she, it	is going to (he's / she's going to)	study write	She **is going to** study English.

Future: *Going to* (Negative)

Subject	*Going to*	Base verb	Example sentence
I	am not going to	learn listen	I **am not going to** learn English.
you, we, they	are not going to	practice read	They **are not going to** read English.
he, she, it	is not going to	speak	She **is not going to** speak English.

Possessive Adjectives

Possession	Possessive adjectives
I have a daughter.	**My** daughter has red hair.
You have a brother.	**Your** brother has green eyes.
He has a mother.	**His** mother has new shoes.
She has an aunt.	**Her** aunt is from San Francisco.
We have children.	**Our** children like sports.
They have parents.	**Their** parents are from China.

Comparative Adjectives

	Question	Answer
Singular	Where is ground beef cheaper?	It's cheaper at Puente Market.
Plural	Where are carrots cheaper?	They're cheaper at Food City.
	Question	**Answer**
Singular	Where is ground beef more expensive?	It's more expensive at Puente Market.
Plural	Where are carrots more expensive?	They're more expensive at Food City.

Comparing Nouns

Subject	*Be*	Comparative adjective	Noun	Example sentence
milk	is	cheaper than	juice	Milk is **cheaper than** juice.
apples	are	cheaper than	bananas	Apples are **cheaper than** bananas.
Subject	***Be***	**Comparative adjective**	**Noun**	**Example sentence**
juice	is	more expensive than	milk	Juice is **more expensive than** milk.
bananas	are	more expensive than	apples	Bananas are **more expensive than** apples.

Possessive Nouns

Possession	Possessive proper nouns
John has a mother.	**John's** mother has brown hair.
Maria has an aunt.	**Maria's** aunt is from San Francisco.
Michael and David have parents.	**Michael and David's** parents are from China.

Possession	Possessive proper nouns
John has a book.	**John's** book is new.
Maria has a pencil.	**Maria's** pencil is yellow.
Michael and David have notebooks.	**Michael and David's** notebooks are green.

Using *from . . . to . . .*

from	Start time	to	End time	Example sentence
from	7:00	to	8:00	He attends school **from** 7:00 **to** 8:00.
	10:30		11:00	He reads **from** 10:30 **to** 11:00.
	5:00		7:00	He practices English **from** 5:00 **to** 7:00.
	8:00		10:00	He watches TV **from** 8:00 **to** 10:00.

How much / How many

	Question	Answer
Noncount	**How much** milk is there?	There is one gallon of milk.
Count	**How many** gallons of milk are there?	There are two gallons of milk.
	How many avocados are there?	There are three avocados.

Question words	Verb	Nouns	Example question
how much (money)	is	the milk	How much **is** the milk?
how much (money)	are	the tomatoes	How much **are** the tomatoes?

Question word	Verb	Example question	Example answer
What	is	**What** is the emergency?	There is a fire! There is an accident. A house is on fire. My father is having a heart attack.
Where	is	**Where** is the emergency?	On First Street. Here in my house. At 1432 W. Palm Street.
Who	is calling is talking is in trouble	**Who** is calling? **Who** is talking? **Who** is in trouble?	John. John. My father, Eric Ludlow.

➤ IRREGULAR SIMPLE PAST VERB LIST

Base form	Simple past form	Base form	Simple past form
be	was, were	make	made
break	broke	pay	paid
buy	bought	put	put
can	could	read	read
choose	chose	run	ran
come	came	say	said
cut	cut	see	saw
do	did	sell	sold
draw	drew	send	sent
drink	drank	shut	shut
drive	drove	sit	sat
eat	ate	sleep	slept
find	found	speak	spoke
get	got	spend	spent
go	went	swim	swam
give	gave	take	took
have	had	teach	taught
hear	heard	understand	understood
hurt	hurt	wake	woke
keep	kept	wear	wore
know	knew	write	wrote

Regular verbs

Base: work   **Infinitive:** to work

Simple present	Present continuous	Simple past	Future
I work	I am working	I worked	I will work
you work	you are working	you worked	you will work
we work	we are working	we worked	we will work
they work	they are working	they worked	they will work
he works	he is working	he worked	he will work
she works	she is working	she worked	she will work
it works	it is working	it worked	it will work

Base: live   **Infinitive:** to live

Simple present	Present continuous	Simple past	Future
I live	I am living	I lived	I will live
you live	you are living	you lived	you will live
we live	we are living	we lived	we will live
they live	they are living	they lived	they will live
he lives	he is living	he lived	he will live
she lives	she is living	she lived	she will live
it lives	it is living	it lived	it will live

Base: study   **Infinitive:** to study

Simple present	Present continuous	Simple past	Future
I study	I am studying	I studied	I will study
you study	you are studying	you studied	you will study
we study	we are studying	we studied	we will study
they study	they are studying	they studied	they will study
he studies	he is studying	he studied	he will study
she studies	she is studying	she studied	she will study
it studies	it is studying	it studied	it will study

Base: stop   **Infinitive:** to stop

Simple present	Present continuous	Simple past	Future
I stop	I am stopping	I stopped	I will stop
you stop	you are stopping	you stopped	you will stop
we stop	we are stopping	we stopped	we will stop
they stop	they are stopping	they stopped	they will stop
he stops	he is stopping	he stopped	he will stop
she stops	she is stopping	she stopped	she will stop
it stops	it is stopping	it stopped	it will stop

Irregular verbs

Base: be	**Infinitive:** to be		
Simple present	**Present continuous**	**Simple past**	**Future**
I am	I am being	I was	I will be
you are	you are being	you were	you will be
we are	we are being	we were	we will be
they are	they are being	they were	they will be
he is	he is being	he was	he will be
she is	she is being	she was	she will be
it is	it is being	it was	it will be

Base: have	**Infinitive:** to have		
Simple present	**Present continuous**	**Simple past**	**Future**
I have	I am having	I had	I will have
you have	you are having	you had	you will have
we have	we are having	we had	we will have
they have	they are having	they had	they will have
he has	he is having	he had	he will have
she has	she is having	she had	she will have
it has	it is having	it had	it will have

Base: go	**Infinitive:** to go		
Simple present	**Present continuous**	**Simple past**	**Future**
I go	I am going	I went	I will go
you go	you are going	you went	you will go
we go	we are going	we went	we will go
they go	they are going	they went	they will go
he goes	he is going	he went	he will go
she goes	she is going	she went	she will go
it goes	it is going	it went	it will go

Base: run	**Infinitive:** to run		
Simple present	**Present continuous**	**Simple past**	**Future**
I run	I am running	I ran	I will run
you run	you are running	you ran	you will run
we run	we are running	we ran	we will run
they run	they are running	they ran	they will run
he runs	he is running	he ran	he will run
she runs	she is running	she ran	she will run
it runs	it is running	it ran	it will run

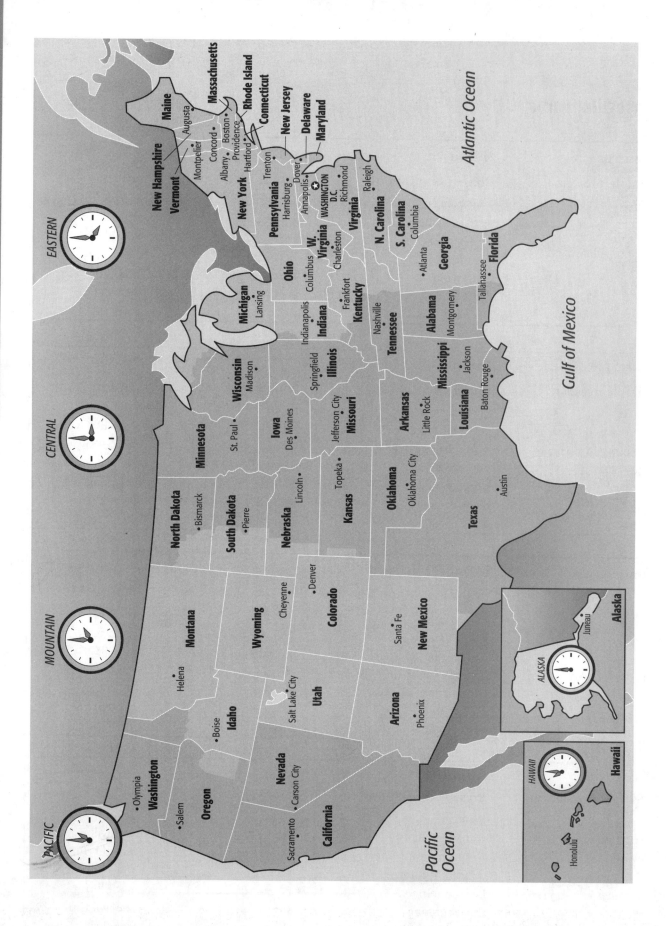

Map of the United States